Lori Driscoll

Electronic Reserve: A Manual and Guide for Library Staff Members

Electronic Reserve: A Manual and Guide for Library Staff Members has been co-published simultaneously as *Journal of Interlibrary Loan, Document Delivery & Information Supply*, Volume 14, Number 1 2003.

Pre-publication REVIEWS, COMMENTARIES, EVALUATIONS . . .

"**I** WISH THIS MANUAL HAD EXISTED FOUR YEARS AGO when we were contemplating purchasing an electronic reserves system for the university library where I work. . . . Or two years ago when we were setting up all of our policies, procedures, and training documentation. . . . THIS IS AN EXCELLENT PUBLICATION and will be an often-consulted resource for those just starting to provide an electronic reserves system and those who have one set up but want to review and revisit our policies and procedures to be certain that we have covered everything efficiently and effectively."

June L. DeWeese, MLS
Head of Access Services
Ellis Library
University of Missouri-Columbia

More pre-publication
REVIEWS, COMMENTARIES, EVALUATIONS . . .

"Librarians who manage or plan to implement electronic reserve services will delight in the number and extent of model e-reserve library policies and procedures provided in this book. Driscoll includes all the players–instructions for faculty who wish to place materials on reserve, guidelines for staff who accept and process reserves, flowcharts to help librarians determine the copyright status of reserve material, and more. THIS IS TRULY HANDS-ON!"

Carrie Russell, MLIS
Copyright Specialist
ALA Office for Information
Technology Policy

"This book is a *vade mecum* for those considering electronic reserve. Its thorough treatment of copyright and fair use, and its many sample policies, forms, and checklists, will be EXTREMELY VALUABLE for anyone wishing to implement such a service, as well as being HIGHLY INFORMATIVE for those who already offer it. Driscoll's practical, experienced approach to electronic reserve is A WELCOME ADDITION TO THE LITERATURE."

William Miller, PhD, MLS
Director of Libraries
Florida Atlantic University

"A USEFUL MANUAL that provides practical information for establishing the service, planning strategically, and establishing workflow. Readers will find the appendix particularly helpful in compiling the documents any new electronic reserve operation will need to have on-hand. COMPREHENSIVE. . . . Boldly explores the varied terrain affecting novice as well as experienced providers of electronic reserve services. . . . Maps the complex landscape of electronic reserve services in academic libraries. For established electronic reserve services, this book TACKLES THE OFTEN-OVERLOOKED AREA OF ASSESSMENT and deftly navigates the murky waters of copyright and fair use."

Leah G. McGinnis, MSLS
Undergraduate Librarian
University of North Carolina
at Chapel Hill

Electronic Reserve:
A Manual and Guide
for Library Staff Members

Electronic Reserve: A Manual and Guide for Library Staff Members has been co-published simultaneously as *Journal of Interlibrary Loan, Document Delivery & Information Supply*, Volume 14, Number 1 2003.

The *Journal of Interlibrary Loan, Document Delivery & Information Supply*™ Monographic "Separates"

(formerly the *Journal of Interlibrary Loan & Information Supply*)*

For information on previous issues of the *Journal of Interlibrary Loan & Information Supply* series, edited by Leslie R. Morris, please contact: The Haworth Press, Inc., 10 Alice Street, Binghamton, NY 13904-1580 USA.

Below is a list of "separates," which in serials librarianship means a special issue simultaneously published as a journal issue or double-issue *and* as a "separate" hardbound monograph. (This is a format which we also call a "DocuSerial.")

"Separates" are published because specialized libraries or professionals may wish to purchase a specific thematic issue by itself in a format which can be separately cataloged and shelved, as opposed to purchasing the journal on an on-going basis. Faculty members may also more easily consider a "separate" for classroom adoption.

"Separates" are carefully classified separately with the major book jobbers so that the journal tie-in can be noted on new book order slips to avoid duplicate purchasing.

You may wish to visit Haworth's Website at . . .

http://www.HaworthPress.com

. . . to search our online catalog for complete tables of contents of these separates and related publications.

You may also call 1-800-HAWORTH (outside US/Canada: 607-722-5857), or Fax 1-800-895-0582 (outside US/Canada: 607-771-0012), or e-mail at:

docdelivery@haworthpress.com

Electronic Reserve: A Manual and Guide for Library Staff Members

Lori Driscoll

Electronic Reserve: A Manual and Guide for Library Staff Members has been co-published simultaneously as *Journal of Interlibrary Loan, Document Delivery & Information Supply*, Volume 14, Number 1 2003.

The Haworth Information Press®
An Imprint of The Haworth Press, Inc.

New York • London • Victoria (AU)
www.HaworthPress.com

Published by

The Haworth Information Press®, 10 Alice Street, Binghamton, NY 13904-1580 USA

The Haworth Information Press® is an imprint of The Haworth Press, Inc., 10 Alice Street, Binghamton, NY 13904-1580 USA.

Electronic Reserve: A Manual and Guide for Library Staff Members has been co-published simultaneously as *Journal of Interlibrary Loan, Document Delivery & Information Supply*, Volume 14, Number 1 2003.

The development, preparation, and publication of this work has been undertaken with great care. However, the publisher, employees, editors, and agents of The Haworth Press and all imprints of The Haworth Press, Inc., including The Haworth Medical Press® and Pharmaceutical Products Press®, are not responsible for any errors contained herein or for consequences that may ensue from use of materials or information contained in this work. Opinions expressed by the author(s) are not necessarily those of The Haworth Press, Inc. With regard to case studies, identities and circumstances of individuals discussed herein have been changed to protect confidentiality. Any resemblance to actual persons, living or dead, is entirely coincidental.

Cover design by Marylouise E. Doyle.

Library of Congress Cataloging-in-Publication Data

Driscoll, Lori.
    Electronic reserve : a manual and guide for library staff members / Lori Driscoll.
      p. cm.
    "Co-published simultaneously as Journal of interlibrary loan, document delivery & information supply, Volume 14, Number 1, 2003."
    Includes bibliographical references and index.
    ISBN 0-7890-1525-0 (alk. paper) – ISBN 0-7890-1526-9 (pbk. : alk. paper)
    1. Electronic reserve collections in libraries–United States. 2. Academic libraries–Electronic reserve collections–United States. 3. Fair use (Copyright)–United States. I. Journal of interlibrary loan, document delivery & information supply. II. Title.
    Z692.R47 D75 2003
    025.6–dc22
                                    2003018582

Indexing, Abstracting & Website/Internet Coverage

This section provides you with a list of major indexing & abstracting services. That is to say, each service began covering this periodical during the year noted in the right column. Most Websites which are listed below have indicated that they will either post, disseminate, compile, archive, cite or alert their own Website users with research-based content from this work. (This list is as current as the copyright date of this publication.)

Abstracting, Website/Indexing Coverage . . . . Year When Coverage Began

- *Academic Abstracts/CD-ROM* **1995**

- *Academic Search: database of 2,000 selected academic serials, updated monthly: EBSCO Publishing* **1995**

- *Academic Search Elite (EBSCO)* **1995**

- *Academic Search Premier (EBSCO)* **1995**

- *CNPIEC Reference Guide: Chinese National Directory of Foreign Periodicals* **1995**

- *Current Cites [Digital Libraries] [Electronic Publishing] [Multimedia & Hypermedia] [Networks & Networking] [General]* **2000**

- *Current Index to Journals in Education* **2001**

- *FRANCIS. INIST/CNRS <http://www.inist.fr>* **1999**

- *IBZ International Bibliography of Periodical Literature <http://www.saur.de>* **1996**

- *Index Guide to College Journals (core list compiled by integrating 48 indexes frequently used to support undergraduate programs in small to medium sized libraries)* **1999**

- *Index to Periodical Articles Related to Law* **1991**

- *Information Reports & Bibliographies* **1991**

(continued)

*Exact start date to come.

(continued)

*Special Bibliographic Notes related to special journal issues
(separates) and indexing/abstracting:*

- indexing/abstracting services in this list will also cover material in any "separate" that is co-published simultaneously with Haworth's special thematic journal issue or DocuSerial. Indexing/abstracting usually covers material at the article/chapter level.
- monographic co-editions are intended for either non-subscribers or libraries which intend to purchase a second copy for their circulating collections.
- monographic co-editions are reported to all jobbers/wholesalers/approval plans. The source journal is listed as the "series" to assist the prevention of duplicate purchasing in the same manner utilized for books-in-series.
- to facilitate user/access services all indexing/abstracting services are encouraged to utilize the co-indexing entry note indicated at the bottom of the first page of each article/chapter/contribution.
- this is intended to assist a library user of any reference tool (whether print, electronic, online, or CD-ROM) to locate the monographic version if the library has purchased this version but not a subscription to the source journal.
- individual articles/chapters in any Haworth publication are also available through the Haworth Document Delivery Service (HDDS).

Electronic Reserve:
A Manual and Guide
for Library Staff Members

CONTENTS

ABOUT THE AUTHOR

Lori Driscoll, MSLS, is Associate University Librarian and Chair of Access Services for the George A. Smathers Libraries at the University of Florida in Gainesville, where she manages the functions of course reserves, circulation, interlibrary loan, stacks maintenance, and the remote storage facility. She has taught undergraduate information studies courses, facilitated workshops on copyright and intellectual freedom, and published articles on access services.

Preface

The information in this guide should not replace the advice of competent legal counsel at individual academic institutions, and the views and opinions stated herein do not necessarily represent those of the University of Florida or the Smathers Libraries. The issues in Part Two examine copyright law in the United States, although libraries throughout the world face similar issues and will benefit from the practical approaches suggested in Part One and the Appendix.

I wish to thank the members of the Circulation Policy Committee who created the original policy documents for the University of Florida Libraries and the electronic reserve staff members that provided comments and suggestions for the sample documents included in the Appendix. Above all, I want to express my appreciation to my husband, Shaun Saxon, who provided editorial advice that was invaluable for the completion of this work.

[Haworth co-indexing entry note]: "Preface." Driscoll, Lori. Co-published simultaneously in *Journal of Interlibrary Loan, Document Delivery & Information Supply* (The Haworth Information Press, an imprint of The Haworth Press, Inc.) Vol. 14, No. 1, 2003, pp. xiii; and: *Electronic Reserve: A Manual and Guide for Library Staff Members* (Lori Driscoll) The Haworth Information Press, an imprint of The Haworth Press, Inc., 2003, pp. xiii. Single or multiple copies of this article are available for a fee from The Haworth Document Delivery Service [1-800-HAWORTH, 9:00 a.m. - 5:00 p.m. (EST). E-mail address: docdelivery@haworth press.com].

xiii

PART ONE:
THE HOW-TO-DO-IT MANUAL
OF ELECTRONIC RESERVE

Chapter 1

Introduction to Electronic Reserve Services

For many years, college and university libraries have been providing course reserve services to support faculty and to provide students wider access to frequently used materials. The "reserve" area may be a special room or simply a reserved collection space behind the circulation desk where faculty may request to place recommended or required readings for their courses. The materials placed on reserve are supplemental and not intended to replace textbooks. Typically, these items have short loan periods so that many students have the opportunity to use them in a brief period of time. Common items for course reserve have been books, photocopies of articles or book chapters, audiovisual materials, and instructor-supplied syllabi, notes, or problem sets. Although a reserve collection provides a greater number of students access to materials, several problems are inherent:

[Haworth co-indexing entry note]: "Introduction to Electronic Reserve Services." Driscoll, Lori. Co-published simultaneously in *Journal of Interlibrary Loan, Document Delivery & Information Supply* (The Haworth Information Press, an imprint of The Haworth Press, Inc.) Vol. 14, No. 1, 2003, pp. 1-5; and: *Electronic Reserve: A Manual and Guide for Library Staff Members* (Lori Driscoll) The Haworth Information Press, an imprint of The Haworth Press, Inc., 2003, pp. 1-5. Single or multiple copies of this article are available for a fee from The Haworth Document Delivery Service [1-800-HAWORTH, 9:00 a.m. - 5:00 p.m. (EST). E-mail address: docdelivery@haworthpress.com].

http://www.haworthpress.com/store/product.asp?sku=J110
10.1300/J110v14n01_01

1

- Loss, damage, or theft of needed course materials results in a long delay of days, weeks, or months to replace them
- Heavy use of items makes it difficult to preserve their condition
- Materials cannot be accessed outside library hours
- Only one student at a time can use an item
- There is limited space behind the Circulation Desk or in a Reserve Room
- A heavy staff workload is involved in the circulation of reserve materials

The evolution of the World Wide Web created an attractive method for distributing materials to students whenever and wherever they want them. Electronic course reserve provides access to supplemental course materials in digital form–both those in existence and those that the library creates–that have been selected by faculty for use by students in their classes. Students can retrieve materials, view them online, download them, and print copies for personal use. Other formats like images and music may also be digitized.

Electronic reserve has the same legal issues regarding copyright as traditional print reserve. Although there have been many attempts to clarify copyright issues, there are no simple rules given by the courts. Despite the overwhelming preference for electronic access to materials by students and faculty, fear of violating copyright law has prevented many libraries from offering electronic course reserve services.

Copyright law primarily exists to balance a creator's right to benefit from the reproduction of a work with the public's right to advance knowledge and expression. The most critical consideration for materials to be included in course reserves, whether printed or electronic, is the determination of fair use. Fair use is determined by considering four factors: purpose of use, nature of the copyrighted work, amount and substantiality of material from original work, and the effect of use on the value of the protected work. Works in the public domain do not require permission for use, but copyright term extensions make it difficult to have a simple rule of thumb to determine when a work has entered the public domain. However, with permission or licensing, the scope and range of materials to be included are limited only by the copyright owners.

The best way to ensure compliance with copyright law is to make it easy for faculty, students, and library staff members to comply. Libraries may assist faculty and students by (1) providing formal and informal instruction about copyright issues, and (2) requesting permission from copyright holders on behalf of faculty to use film text, images, audio, and video. Policies and procedures developed in consultation with faculty and administrators will help library staff members in this process. Checklists and forms can ensure consistency among staff.

As of August 2001, only 50 of more than 120 members of the Association of Research Libraries offered an electronic reserve service (Rosedale, 2001). Digital technologies have transformed higher education, and distance education has diversified the student body. Along with these changes, the expectations of students and faculty are challenging the library to evolve and meet their demands.

The Pew Internet & American Life Project (Jones et al., 2002) reports that college students are heavy users of the Internet. Eighty-five percent (85%) of college students own their own computers. The Internet is a part of students' daily routine, like telephones and television, and is used to communicate with professors and classmates, do research, and access library materials. Unfortunately, nearly three-quarters (73%) of respondents say that they use the Internet more than the library for information searching. And with faculty using the Web as a course tool for distance as well as onsite classes, electronic course reserve services are more important than ever.

Users highly value the convenience of electronic reserve. Sellen and Hazard (2001) and other case reports confirm an overwhelmingly positive reaction to electronic course reserve. Students comment that electronic reserve materials are accessible, convenient, easy to use, and unrestricted to the library. Students also noted that courses with electronic reserve offer more materials than those with traditional reserve; and the students reported feeling that electronic reserve generally improves these courses. Electronic reserve includes the following advantages:

- 24-hour, 7-days-a-week access to materials, regardless of the hours the library is open
- Materials are available to students anywhere, on or off campus
- Distance learning programs have greater access to library materials
- Gain space once used for shelving traditional reserves
- Service hours and locations are greatly expanded with minimal impact on staffing levels
- Students no longer accrue hourly fines for returning materials late

The technology for electronic course reserve has existed for over a decade, but libraries continue to grapple with copyright issues surrounding the service. Visionaries sought to digitize materials in an accessible database that could be processed through the integrated library automation system. In 1994, San Diego State University, Colorado State University, and Duke University attended a forum sponsored by the Association of Research Libraries (ARL). Each institution approached electronic course reserve differently: one worked with the campus bookstore to seek copyright permission to use anything; one only used items that did not require copyright clearance; and another claimed all use was fair use and did not require permission. With the emergence of the Web as a means of access to electronic reserve collections, new modules that integrate with vendors' library automation systems and new stand-alone electronic reserve systems came on the market. Due to the complexity of copyright clearance for electronic reserve services, however, most libraries continue to have both print and electronic reserve collections.

When establishing the service, the library must determine how use will be interpreted as "fair." This determination will fall somewhere between the claim that all use in electronic reserve is fair and the opposite approach of seeking permission for everything. There is no standardized approach to managing electronic reserve services. Each library is affected by institutional copyright policies, and the level of staffing and type of system implemented are contingent upon available resources.

A common fear is that electronic reserve services will make it easier to use materials in excess of what would be considered fair use. However, the faculty has produced most materials on reserve themselves. In Kristof's 1999 study, the most common types of materials placed on electronic reserve were instructor-produced course notes, sample tests, and exercises or problem sets. Other materials include links to web pages, syllabi, homework solutions, and student-produced materials. Of course, journal articles and book chapters were also used, and as libraries acquire more materials in electronic format, links to electronic books and full text journal articles in library databases are likely to increase.

Another study conducted by the North East Research Libraries consortium (NERL) and reported by Okerson (2001, September 1) attempted to identify frequently taught information in order to create a more collaborative model of electronic course reserve. The project did not confirm the hypothesis that many institutions teach the same titles over and over, which would require copyright permission and most likely fees for each use. Of the many items discussed from the study, the following points are of interest to electronic reserve:

1. The reserve readings in the study were more likely to focus on secondary literature rather than an original work. This finding suggests that students continue to purchase textbooks and major

works covered in the courses and that reserves are used to supplement those materials.

2. Reserve reading lists are highly customized and individualized, even for very standard undergraduate courses in history and literature. This discovery indicates that individual instructors utilize different materials, so items are less likely to need copyright clearance for all sections of a course.
3. Anthologies of critical literature about works by eminent authors appeared frequently in reserve lists. Electronic course reserve provides a valuable service to faculty and students by incorporating the relevant readings for a course into a convenient access point, similar to anthologies.
4. Reserve services, whether traditional or electronic, are labor-intensive. Traditional reserve items take less time to process initially, but are circulated frequently and are therefore handled frequently by staff members. Electronic reserve items take more time to process initially, but are not handled again by staff members until the end of the term.

In today's academic environment, library reserve services now compete with faculty web pages or courseware reserve products like Blackboard and WebCT. Faculty often incorporate copyrighted materials into their own multimedia presentations. It is important that the institution comply with copyright law. Learning about copyright issues and developing sound policies and procedures will help library staff members in this process.

Industry guidelines and policy statements exist to guide libraries in crafting copyright policies. When acting within the bounds of fair use and taking reasonable measures to protect the interests of copyright owners, nonprofit educational institutions are unlikely to infringe copyright. Most institutions feel that using some set of guidelines will at least show "good faith." Staff members want common sense policies and procedures that are easy to adopt.

Changes in the law are so frequent that it is critical for library staff members to stay informed. Uncertainty is the only certainty regarding copyright law. This book discusses the relevant legislation for electronic reserve services in academic libraries and provides general guidelines and practices for library staff members to plan, implement, and evaluate an effective electronic reserve service.

Chapter 2

Getting Started

There is no standardized approach to managing electronic reserve services. Each library is affected by institutional copyright policies, and the level of staffing and type of system implemented are contingent upon available resources. Electronic reserve policies and procedures will reflect these factors.

Libraries that implement electronic course reserve often experience a two-fold increase in use of the service. Although the demand increases, it is common for the existing reserve staff members to take on the new service without additional support. Therefore it is crucial to examine the system, staffing, and workflow upfront. The feasibility of providing reserve services should be determined, including both short-term and long-term costs. Staffing levels may include library technical assistants, student assistants, an electronic reserve coordinator, an electronic reserve librarian or access services librarian, and an automation librarian or network services manager. Also consider the availability of funding for other costs such as royalty payments and equipment purchases.

STRATEGIC PLANNING

Strategic planning is a way to define and assess organizational goals in a constantly changing environment where decisions and actions shape future objectives. The "strategic" part incorporates organiza-

[Haworth co-indexing entry note]: "Getting Started." Driscoll, Lori. Co-published simultaneously in *Journal of Interlibrary Loan, Document Delivery & Information Supply* (The Haworth Information Press, an imprint of The Haworth Press, Inc.) Vol. 14, No. 1, 2003, pp. 7-25; and: *Electronic Reserve: A Manual and Guide for Library Staff Members* (Lori Driscoll) The Haworth Information Press, an imprint of The Haworth Press, Inc., 2003, pp. 7-25. Single or multiple copies of this article are available for a fee from The Haworth Document Delivery Service [1-800-HAWORTH, 9:00 a.m. - 5:00 p.m. (EST). E-mail address: docdelivery@ haworthpress.com].

tional objectives and resources into the planning process. The questions below can help an organization shape electronic course reserve goals:

- Does an electronic course reserve service fall within the mission of the library?
- Who will be the users?
- What are their needs?
- How will the service meet these needs?

Strategic planning for electronic reserve should include articulating a specific vision and mission for the service. Most often, the goals of electronic reserve services are to enhance instructional services, provide 24-hour, 7-days-a-week access to course materials, decrease theft or mutilation of needed materials, and reduce staff member involvement in the circulation of materials. A well-run service can provide opportunities for the library to partner with faculty and may mitigate the stress that students feel when needed items are not available.

Assessing what is happening outside of the institution is just as important as monitoring the service itself; for example, would the service be redundant with courseware or services being offered by other campus instructional units? The next steps would include developing goals and objectives for the service and measuring progress toward those goals for continuous improvement. Another important task is developing specifications for the system that is needed. Once the system has been chosen, policies and procedures can be drafted for library staff members, faculty, and students. At this time, standardized forms and letters can be developed. In order to evaluate the effectiveness of service, at least one assessment tool should be developed, and workflow should be re-evaluated continuously. Other ongoing activities include educating staff members and users and communicating internally and externally about the service. Staff member training should be considered an ongoing process due to procedural improvements and staff member attrition.

STAFFING

Who will do the work? Will the same staff members currently providing traditional reserve services be assigned these additional responsibilities? Will faculty create electronic documents and procure permissions, or will the library manage that process? There are no standard practices; services depend in large part on the library's mission, available resources such as staffing and speed of equipment, volume of materials to handle, and even the system used.

It is important for public service desk staff members to demonstrate effective communication skills in their interactions with faculty and students. Having clear instructions and guidelines for all staff members to follow when accepting submissions from faculty will save time for both the reserve staff members and faculty later on. Public services staff members should know the policies and clearly explain those when necessary. Students may need assistance finding and using electronic course reserve materials, especially if full-text databases do not permit a direct link to the article.

Reserve unit staff members need to be flexible, adjusting workflow to accommodate the cyclical nature of the tasks. In addition to following policies and procedures, they need to exercise good judgment. Technological proficiency will vary, and there may or may not be a steep learning curve depending on the particular reserve system used.

Different levels of staffing may be necessary for the specific tasks involved in the electronic reserve service:

- Maintaining system hardware and software
- Accepting materials
- Reviewing materials for completeness
- Searching bibliographic databases
- Identifying materials that need permission
- Obtaining needed permissions from publishers, authors, or the Copyright Clearance Center (CCC)
- Creating and maintaining a database of items that require permission
- Coordinating requests and tracking for all reserve units
- Monitoring the budget
- Processing invoices
- Scanning or otherwise reformatting materials
- Uploading and maintaining files on the server
- Entering item information into the reserves system
- Finding alternatives when costs are prohibitive
- Educating faculty, students, and other staff members regarding copyright issues relevant to reserves
- Supervising the work of other staff members in the unit.

Electronic Reserve Coordinator

Although it is important for reserve staff members to have basic knowledge of copyright law, at least one person in the unit should have a more advanced understanding of copyright issues. This person should be able to communicate this information to others and to stay current with changes in legislation. Even when the faculty procure permission, the library has a responsibility to monitor compliance if the library maintains the materials.

Many institutions have a coordinator who manages the system of record keeping. This staff member is responsible for monitoring the compliance with library policies, tracking usage, requesting permissions, and paying royalty fees. The coordinator may track copyright holders who take a long time to respond or who repeatedly deny permission, managing this process with a database. As the resident "expert" on electronic reserve, this person may also work with whoever negotiates electronic database licenses to allow linking to full-text.

In order to define staff responsibilities, it may be helpful to think about the specific competencies required for each activity that takes place in the electronic reserve process. The following sets of competencies for non-supervisory and supervisory staff were developed from Avery et al. (2001), Niederlander (1998), and the Tampa Bay Library Consortium (2000).

Non-Supervisory Staff Competencies

Accountability

- Demonstrate initiative and accept responsibility for actions, results, and risks.

Communication

Oral Communications

- Demonstrate effective listening and questioning skills.
- Express ideas and facts in a clear, organized, and convincing manner in a style, tone, and level appropriate to the audience and the occasion.
- Listen to others and show an understanding of what they are saying.

Written Communications

- Express facts and ideas in writing in a clear, convincing, and organized manner that is appropriate to the audience and occasion.
- Transmit information accurately and understandably.

Flexibility

- Be willing to adapt to and participate in change.
- Handle a variety of tasks while adapting personal styles and preferences to the demands of the situation.
- Maintain a positive attitude during challenging times.

Innovation

- Look for opportunities to apply new and evolving ideas, methods, designs, and technologies.
- Be willing to take risks, experiment, and make mistakes.

Interpersonal

- Build positive work relationships and partnerships at all organizational levels with sensitivity to how individuals, organizational units, and cultures function and react.
- Treat coworkers and patrons with honesty, respect, and fairness.
- Attempt to resolve conflict situations.
- Honor different cultures and values.

Organizational

- Know the mission and role of the library.
- Understand the responsibilities and relationships between the different departments in the library, such as public services, technical services, and administration.

Personal Development

- Seek out and participate in continuing education opportunities in order to keep skills current and broaden knowledge.
- Integrate new techniques and methodologies into everyday practice.
- Be open to self-evaluation and thoughtful evaluation by superiors, peers, and customers in order to become a better employee.

Problem-Solving

- Collect information and draw logical conclusions.
- Use sound judgment in making recommendations and decisions.

Resource Management

- Demonstrate a consistent focus on minimizing expenses while maximizing results.

Service Attitude

- Demonstrate a commitment to serving patrons.
- Treat others with respect while addressing and meeting their needs.

Teamwork

- Value the contributions of others.
- Strive to be a positive example for others to follow.
- Model and encourage high standards of honesty, integrity, trust, openness, and respect for others.
- Work with others to achieve common organizational goals in a spirit of collegiality and mutual respect.

Technical Expertise

- Demonstrate basic skills in the use of appropriate computer software and hardware applications for library reserve functions and services.
- Understand how reserves are organized and accessed within the library.

Manager or Team Leader Competencies

Accountability

- Take responsibility for actions.
- Monitor electronic reserve service and activities.
- Encourage others to take ownership of work, services, and results.

Communication

Oral Communications

- Demonstrate effective listening and questioning skills.
- Express ideas and facts in a clear, organized, and convincing manner in a style, tone, and level appropriate to the audience and the occasion.

- Listen to others and show an understanding of what they are saying.
- Facilitate open exchange of ideas.

Written Communications

- Express facts and ideas in writing in a clear, convincing, and organized manner that is appropriate to the audience and occasion.
- Transmit information accurately and understandably.
- Review and critique the writing of others in a constructive manner.

Flexibility

- Be willing to adjust behavior and work methods in response to management priorities, multiple demands, new information, changing conditions, unexpected obstacles, and ambiguity.
- Demonstrate openness to new ideas and approaches.
- Respond constructively to reversals and setbacks by identifying lessons learned and looking for other opportunities.

Innovation

- Demonstrate insights, innovative solutions, and non-traditional approaches to improve organizational effectiveness.
- Create an environment that encourages, recognizes, and rewards risk-taking, creativity, and innovation.
- Design and implement new or innovative programs or processes.

Interpersonal

- Build positive work relationships and partnerships at all organizational levels with sensitivity to how individuals, organizational units, and cultures function and react.
- Treat coworkers and patrons with honesty, respect, and fairness.
- Attempt to resolve conflict situations.
- Understand how cultures differ and how these differences impact work behavior.
- Negotiate mutually beneficial solutions to problems and conflicts.
- Persuade others to consider alternative points of view.
- Maintain a professional demeanor in stressful and difficult situations.

Leadership

- Set and model high performance standards characterized by integrity.
- Earn the trust and respect of others by coaching, inspiring, and empowering teams of people to achieve strategic objectives.
- Create an environment that encourages and rewards cooperation, collective problem-solving and participative decision-making.
- Value the contributions of others and help them to achieve their full potential.
- Effectively develop networks and build alliances with key individuals or groups.

Organizational

- Articulate and actively support the library's vision in a way that causes employees at all levels to understand the goals, values, and objectives.
- Develop and maintain supportive relationships across the organization.
- Anticipate and predict internal and external changes, trends, and influences in order to effectively allocate resources and implement appropriate library initiatives.

Personal Development

- Invest time and energy in self-development and growth.
- Integrate the acquisition of knowledge or skills into daily work.

Problem Solving

- Make difficult or controversial decisions when necessary.
- Exercise good judgment by making sound and well-informed decisions.
- Recognize, define, and analyze problems and issues.
- Obtain relevant data before making a decision.
- Develop alternative solutions and plans to solve problems.
- Use qualitative and quantitative data and analytical tools in problem solving.

Resource Management

- Develop and manage convenient and accessible electronic reserve services that promote and support the organization's mission and strategic direction.

- Use appropriate business and management approaches to communicate the value of electronic reserve services to decision makers in the organization.
- Take an active role in recruiting, training, and developing staff members.
- Identify performance expectations, assess employee performance, give timely feedback, and conduct formal performance appraisals.
- Take timely and appropriate corrective actions with employees.
- Support programs and activities that promote employee well being and balance.

Service Attitude

- Identify and anticipate the needs of users and integrate user and other stakeholder needs and expectations into the development and delivery of services.
- Establish and utilize feedback systems to meet user requirements and expectations.

Technological Expertise

- Appropriately apply policies, procedures, and standards related to electronic reserve.
- Ensure that staff members are trained and capable in new technology.
- Strategically integrate technologies into the workflow to improve unit effectiveness.

ELECTRONIC RESERVE SYSTEM

The planning phase involves the selection of the electronic reserve system. The library should assess needs and analyze available resources. The next step is to develop specifications that are unique to the library's particular needs and resources. ARL libraries (Kristof, 1999) ranked functionality as the highest consideration, followed by system compatibility, cost, Web accessibility, integration with the online public access catalog (OPAC), intellectual property management and references from current customers.

Particular features may be absolutely vital while others are less critical but helpful to the functioning of the electronic reserve service. The three critical components to an electronic reserve system are scanning, indexing, and maintaining the files. Helpful components include copyright management, reporting statistics, and user authentication. Finally, in order to accomplish critical tasks, the electronic reserve service will need at least one workstation and scanner with scanning software.

Software

Identify the software features that are absolutely necessary for the library's needs.

- Scans or otherwise creates files
  - Handles a variety of file types (PDF, DOC, XLS, PPT, ZIP, etc.) and links
- Indexes the materials in an accessible system
  - Includes forms for entry of course and bibliographic data
  - Database driven, creates pages dynamically
  - Requires information to be entered only once but can be used in multiple ways
- Maintains the materials
  - Archives the materials
  - Items for courses can be removed at end of a specified time period, e.g., the end of the semester, without intervention
  - Materials can be retrieved for subsequent semesters
- Facilitates access
  - Web-based
  - Allows the creation of class 'accounts'
  - Integrates with the OPAC
  - Authenticates users for access
  - Makes all file formats accessible
  - If additional software is required for access, it is freely available, e.g., Adobe Acrobat Reader or RealPlayer
- Administrative management
  - Records and calculates a variety of statistics
  - Tracks user behavior
  - Enables staff members in the searching of specific readings in addition to courses and instructors
  - Logs problem areas
  - Provides some level of system security

Is additional software necessary; and if so, how does it integrate with the system?

The most popular scanning software in ARL libraries (Kristof, 1999) was the Adobe Acrobat suite, including Capture, Distiller, Exchange, and so on, followed by Adobe Photoshop and OmniPage.

Hardware

- What are the hardware requirements?
  - Platform that is compatible with other systems
  - Server (does not necessarily need to be dedicated; will depend on how many documents are stored)
  - Back up server or tape system
  - Computer workstation for staff
  - High volume flatbed scanner (automatic feeder is useful for $8.5'' \times 11''$ photocopies)

Other System Considerations

- Price
- Ease of use for library staff members as well as faculty and students
- Customer support
- Reputation of the vendor: how do other customers feel about the implementation of the product and ongoing support?

There are basically two systems options to consider: developing your own system in-house or partnering with a vendor. The partnership may consist of contracting with an outside service, integrating an electronic reserve module with the existing library automation system or courseware product, or purchasing a system that is complete and ready to install. The main differences among the choices involve staff time, cost, and customizability. Libraries that do not have the technical staff to create and manage an in-house system may be interested in the options offered by vendors.

In-house systems require local technical expertise and significant programming resources initially, but may offer cost savings over time. These customized systems may be created quickly without too much administrative involvement, and the design is locally controlled. However, adding more robust features requires longer development time and increases costs. Also, technological support for staff members may be limited.

Libraries often prefer the ease of use and technical support offered by systems that have been specifically designed for electronic reserves, especially for staff members with little or no technical knowledge that need to learn the system quickly. These systems may offer fuller features and enhancements with the release of upgrades, and vendors usually offer at least some level of technical support. The disadvantages are that the selection process may be long, the costs may be higher, and product features may not match institutional requirements.

Many libraries have implemented Docutek's ERes product for its features and support. Other libraries utilize standard courseware products like Blackboard or WebCT when the institution offers courses through those systems; however, courseware products are designed for faculty and usually lack copyright management features. Library automation system vendors are continuing to develop electronic reserve modules that integrate with their OPACs.

In Kristof's study, homegrown systems were favored by ARL libraries. Some reasons may include such features as customization, integration with the OPAC, patron authentication, and copyright tracking. There are reports of libraries that utilize standard database software like Microsoft Access and Lotus Notes to create an interface. Some libraries are utilizing OCLC SiteSearch now that it is open source software. There is an excellent discussion of implementing a homegrown system at Southern Illinois University-Carbondale by Nackerud (1999), available at http://www.ala.org/acrl/nackerud.pdf; see also FreeReserves Open Source at http://www.lib.umn.edu/san/freereserves/.

POLICIES

When establishing the service, the library must determine how use will be interpreted as "fair." This determination will fall somewhere between the claim that all use in electronic reserve is fair and the opposite approach of seeking permission for everything. As Jensen (1993, p. 42) notes, "Nothing in section 107 limits copying to a single copy for a single user . . . Furthermore, it says, 'including' not limited to 'classroom use.' " Paying for everything is very safe; but in doing so, the library is giving up its rights under fair use. Also, when permission is sought the first time an item is used, the library risks denial or may be asked to pay royalty fees on something that could have been used freely.

When establishing policies and procedures, the library should determine the copyright comfort level at the greater institution. A library that claims all use is fair use is less likely to be supported by an institution that takes a conservative legal stance on the issue. But, as Melamut et al. (2000) have so aptly stated, "As part of the educational process, the library is in a position to guide institutional policies and should be ready to recommend what it has determined to be the best course of action for protecting rights and reducing liability" (p. 18). This must be a collaborative effort because individual faculty members, the library, and the institution are liable in infringement claims.

Policies should clarify the responsibilities of students, faculty, the information technology unit, and the library. Who secures permissions and who pays? Who is responsible for the copyright education program? Print and electronic materials should be specifically addressed, as well as what is legal, permissible, illegal, and impermissible. Record retention procedures should be clearly outlined.

The library should next determine the scope of the service. Will everything except hard materials like books and videos be entirely electronic? What formats will be acceptable for text, sound, images: PDF, MP3, PowerPoint, URLs? What will not be accepted, such as consumables (e.g., workbooks and study guides), course packs, or textbooks? Will you seek permission to use these? What about exams, notes, assignments, syllabi, presentations, journals, links to course web pages, scanned articles, and scanned chapters? Will you offer to seek permission to use these items and put them on reserve if the publisher grants permission?

There are four factors that must be considered when determining fair use, but the law does not require that all four be present. One is not more important than another and other factors may also be considered.

1. *Use.* Non-commercial, educational use such as a nonprofit organization using it for teaching, scholarship, or research, or use for the purposes of criticism, commentary, parody, reporting, or some other transformative use are strengthened by limiting access to enrolled students. The material should contain a notice of copyright.
2. *Nature.* Materials should be more factual than creative and not consumables (workbooks, exercises or problems, standardized tests). Senate Report Number 94-473 states, "Copying shall not be used to create or to replace or substitute for anthologies, compilations or collective works. Such replacement or substitution may occur whether copies of various works or excerpts there from are accumulated or reproduced and used separately" (p. 63).
3. *Amount.* Balance both quality and quantity. Quantity is measured relative to the length of the work and the amount needed to meet the educational purpose. This stipulation indicates that longer works should not be copied. The quality is also important; if the

amount copied is very small but is the heart of the work, it may not be a fair use. General arbitrary guidelines are to photocopy no more than an entire article, an entire chapter from a book, or an entire poem without permission, and to seek permission for requests above those limits from the same work.

4. *Effect.* Limiting access to and placing technological controls on reproduction of works lessens adverse effects on the market. Because the effect of photocopying should not be detrimental, electronic reserve should not replace the purchase of the original work when that is feasible. The scope of market effect has been broadened to include income from subscriptions, licensing agents, selling excerpts, and royalty fees.

Eligibility for and methods of accessing the system should be included in policy documentation. Most libraries limit access to electronic reserve materials through password protection or IP-authentication. The appropriate method for limiting access will depend on the technology available to the institution. Individual passwords can be tied to student registration status or each course can share a password. Document whether the library or faculty is responsible for distributing the password. Materials on reserve should be retrieved only by course number or instructor name. Access can be limited to workstations accessible to enrolled students only, such as in the library or through a proxy server. Existing laws and guidelines indicate the need to utilize the most secure technology available to an institution.

Policies should explain relevant copyright law to faculty and students. Including an "I accept these terms" message that precedes the online item reinforces the library's position. Provide information to faculty about the limits of fair use and copyright issues in course reserves, and document faculty responsibilities. Unless a work is free from copyright restrictions, permission must be obtained from the copyright holder for a work to remain on electronic reserve longer than one semester. If any fees are charged for copies, an explanation of those fees should also be included.

FACULTY

The faculty plays a major role in the planning of the service and the development of policies and procedures. Factors that should be assessed when planning the service include the institutional support for distance education, the technological proficiency of faculty and students, and other competing instructional resources like courseware products in which the readings are processed by the faculty directly. Policies should define the scope of faculty control over materials throughout the process of account creation, submission of files, password distribution, and permission procurement. Faculty may want to play a greater role in the reserve process, but many also want the library to continue to serve as a central management and access point, to provide training for users, and to manage copyright compliance. The institutional climate should impact the decision about who is ultimately responsible for seeking permissions: individual faculty, reserve unit staff members, or a specific permissions coordinator.

One of the most important factors in a successful electronic reserve service is faculty compliance with procedures to ensure that materials are available when the students need them. An ARL survey found that more than half of reserve lists are submitted after the start of the semester, and faculty often bring in materials even later in the term, thinking that these can be scanned and made available immediately for student use. Libraries can counter this by informing faculty of the requirements for copyright compliance: a complete citation, work in the original format, and the copyright statement from the publisher. Libraries can help faculty prepare complete citations for their readings on course syllabi. Submission policies and procedures should clarify deadlines, acceptable methods of submission, types of materials accepted, formats, restrictions on file size, or other parameters. In addition to faculty responsibilities, submission policies and procedures should state what the faculty should expect from the service, such as turnaround time.

The University of North Carolina includes a fair use worksheet as part of the reserve materials submission form completed by faculty (see http://www.northcarolina.edu/legal/copyright/PrimerFairUseWorksheet. cfm). It is similar to the Fair Use Scale shown in Chapter Two, but the faculty member analyzes fair use of items before submitting them to the library electronic reserve unit. Individual faculty members are responsible for maintaining these records for three years.

TRAINING

Although it initially takes significant time and effort, a training program is essential to the success of the service. Training is necessary for staff members who will work with electronic reserves, faculty who will submit materials, and students who will use those materials. There are eight stages in the creation of a program.

I. Analyze needs

Identify specific training needs. Develop specific training goals for the trainee, the unit, and the library. Conduct continuous training and staff development to respond to changes based on feedback, policy interpretations, and technology, as well as staff turnover. Each unit should have a resident expert trainer to serve as a resource.

II. Describe tasks

What work must be done? Describe each task that must occur for the flow of materials in the unit. It is not necessary at this point to determine who will do what, only what tasks must be accomplished and in what order.

III. Analyze tasks

Who must perform each task? Determine vital skills for each task and critical areas that require a greater level of accountability, judgment, and commitment. These activities should be reserved for core employees. Clearly define each job with a description of duties and core competencies.

IV. Write training objectives

What should the employee be able to do after training? The training approach should be problem-centered. In addition to learning a job, another goal of training is to make connections between the employee and supervisor and the employee and other staff members. Develop an orientation checklist to ensure that all objectives have been met through the course of training.

V. Develop pretests, if necessary

Do you need to test for core competencies before training begins? A thorough training program can be adapted to fit the particular needs of each trainee, and these needs can be assessed from pretests.

VI. Formulate a strategy

Both practical and theoretical instruction is necessary for an understanding of policies and how individual procedures fit into the overall process. Adults learn by doing, yet there are differences in pace, style, and motivation. Recognize these diverse learning styles and utilize a variety of methods including manuals, classes, individualized tutoring, self-paced tutorials, and videos. Build on the trainee's current experiences and skills.

VII. Sequence learning activities

Who will train? Where? When? How often? What materials are necessary? Plan specific activities based on the formulated strategy.

VIII. Develop materials

- Training manual
- Formal class instruction
- Informal 1:1 instruction
- Self-paced tutorial
- Video
- Handout/"cheat-sheet"
- Checklist

Because staff members will not be the only users of the system, instruction for students and faculty is also important. The eight steps above may be modified to develop objectives, strategies, and materials to inform faculty and students about using electronic reserve. Handouts and "Help" documentation for users at the point of entry into the system are common training materials. Other approaches include providing classroom instruction and installing a dedicated workstation located near the reserve unit where staff members can demonstrate and teach access to users.

PUBLICITY

Publicity and user training are very closely related in electronic reserve services. In addition to announcing the service, it is important to include "how-to" information. Assist faculty in the submission of materials and guide students through accessing the readings. Access to the service should be prominently available from the main page of the library's web site. Other methods for announcing the service include a "What's New" note on the web site, flyers posted or mailed, e-mail, announcements at faculty meetings or to faculty liaisons, and press releases to campus publications.

ASSESSMENT

Ongoing assessment and evaluation is essential to strategic planning, but fewer than half of the ARL libraries surveyed in 1999 had an evaluation process for their electronic reserve services. In the beginning, establishing measurable performance goals and indicators assist in planning for resource allocation. To monitor performance:

1. Develop a list of tasks,
2. Specify the order in which those tasks are performed,
3. Determine who will perform each task, and
4. Set the deadline for completion of each task.

By reviewing the dates that tasks were completed in addition to the other measures of performance, a library can learn how effectively the service utilizes resources.

In the assessment phase, a library measures four factors:

- Input (resources)
- Process (activities)
- Output (service provided)
- Outcome (impact).

Measures should be practical and relevant. It's also helpful if they are simple, fast, and inexpensive. These factors will make it easier for staff members to assist in gathering data. In order to assess progress toward goals, all stakeholders in the service must be identified including library staff members, students, and faculty. Measure what is important to these stakeholders: time, money, quality, and so on. Definitions of success should be based on the objectives identified in the planning process. Develop criteria for measuring these objectives to determine success. Typical measures for electronic reserve services examine three areas:

1. *Satisfaction*: success, ease of use, satisfaction with experience
2. *Materials*: availability, quality, quantity
3. *Use*: circulation, visits (including remote 'visits' to web pages).

Processes for review should be meaningful to the institution.

- What savings will be gained by placing more responsibility on faculty? If faculty are required to secure permissions, is it too much of a hassle? Will quality suffer? Will compliance suffer?

- Do people want this service? Is faculty using it? Are students?
- How well is the system working? Is it fast? Easy to use? What is the quality of the product?
- How does the electronic service compare to print reserve? Are articles read more by students? Are students spending more time reading electronic articles than those in print?

Indicators of these measures may vary by stakeholders. As the primary users, the perceptions of students are critical. Indicators should be related to lack of complaints, speed of retrieval, quality of items, and ease of use. The faculty has different expectations. They are usually willing to wait for longer download times in exchange for better quality scans, although timeliness and convenience are still important.

The next step is to gather the data needed to assess performance. One way to gather data is through unobtrusive observation–just listening to what students and faculty say about the service and reading anecdotal comments and suggestions. A manager can also observe what work is getting done and what isn't. Other unobtrusive methods include monitoring usage, costs, processing time, quantity of documents that are available, number of 'help' calls or e-mails, web page hits, and system-generated statistics.

Questionnaires may be administered onsite, online, or through other channels such as the telephone and direct mail. Surveys are good for measuring attitudes and preferences, but not necessarily behaviors. Sampling and distribution methods may affect the validity of the results. The survey instrument should consist of open-ended as well as rated or ranked questions that are written clearly and without jargon (see example *Course Reserve Satisfaction Survey*). Questionnaires can consist of a "Comments" link from within the service, an e-mail survey to faculty and/or students, or a printed user survey that is distributed in class. Interviews are another form of questionnaire that may be conducted with individuals or through focus groups. The personalized contact from interviews typically yields a better response rate and allows for clarification of responses, but interviews are time-consuming and require a skilled interviewer.

The results of this assessment can be used to assist planning and decision-making, improve customer service perception, provide performance feedback for staff members, and justify current and future resource allocation.

Chapter 3

Ongoing Processes

Once the electronic reserve service has been established, many of the initial activities will become ongoing activities: training faculty and students, publicizing and evaluating the service, and implementing changes based on data analysis. Workflow will be cyclical throughout the semester as the unit receives incoming materials, processes permissions documentation, and corresponds with faculty about the maintenance of course reserve items.

WORKFLOW

System features will impact the efficiency of the unit's workflow. Coding in HTML, distributing passwords, documenting the permissions process in a Microsoft Access database, and so on are activities that can consume a lot of staff time. To improve processing efficiency and the users' perception of service quality, prioritize each activity. The operating procedures should specify

- What file format should be used (TIFF, PDF, etc.)?
- The standard resolution of images
- Maximum file sizes
- Whether or not optical character recognition (OCR) should be used (or in what circumstances)

[Haworth co-indexing entry note]: "Ongoing Processes." Driscoll, Lori. Co-published simultaneously in *Journal of Interlibrary Loan, Document Delivery & Information Supply* (The Haworth Information Press, an imprint of The Haworth Press, Inc.) Vol. 14, No. 1, 2003, pp. 27-34; and: *Electronic Reserve: A Manual and Guide for Library Staff Members* (Lori Driscoll) The Haworth Information Press, an imprint of The Haworth Press, Inc., 2003, pp. 27-34. Single or multiple copies of this article are available for a fee from The Haworth Document Delivery Service [1-800-HAWORTH, 9:00 a.m. - 5:00 p.m. (EST). E-mail address: docdelivery@ haworthpress.com].

10.1300/J110v14n01_03   *27*

The advantages of using OCR include the ability of a browser to display the document without additional software, smaller file size, and the creation of a searchable document that can also be read by text-only browsers. The disadvantages of OCR can include imprecise reproductions and inaccurate translation of characters. These shortfalls mean that staff members spend more time reviewing the document and correcting errors. PDF is not searchable but is accurately reproduced on the screen or in print using freely available software. Although the file size is larger, the document is true to the original work and scanning is less labor-intensive.

One method of prioritizing workflow is to schedule the scanning of particular documents, as they are needed, according to the assignment dates provided by instructors, rather than scanning all items for each course in the order that they are submitted. Reserve units that have a large number of staff members working varied schedules may want to use a scanning flowchart or checklist so that one staff member may complete a job started by another staff member that was interrupted. Additional techniques to streamline workflow include minimizing redundancy, eliminating duplicate entry of information, using templates, and receiving requests in electronic format to prevent re-keying. A good example of staff documentation, a document created by Wellesley College Information Services that shows staff members how to use Adobe Acrobat to scan electronic reserve material, is available at http://www.wellesley.edu/Computing/Acrobat/E-Reserves/e-reserve-scanning-fujitsu.html (see Appendix).

General Overview of Electronic Reserve Procedures

- A faculty member requests to place an item on course reserve. The request is submitted physically at a public service desk or virtually through an online form or email message.
- At the point of receipt, a staff member reviews the request for legibility, complete course information, citation, and a publisher copyright statement. A reserve item authored by a student or faculty member must be accompanied by a signed release from the author. To save time later on, this staff member collects additional information needed for permission at the time of submission.
- The request is forwarded to reserve staff and they determine whether the item may be scanned into electronic reserve or if it must be forwarded for copyright permission.
- When the item can be added, a staff member creates an account and a course page for each instructor.

- The reserve staff members search the library's resources for ownership and electronic availability.
- Staff members scan the document according to library guidelines.
- A library copyright notice is included with every document in addition to the required copyright statement from the publication.
- Staff members check the quality of the scan, then crop, rotate, or re-scan as necessary.
- Staff members then save the file and upload it to the electronic reserve system.
- Staff members enter the bibliographic record or item information into the system and create links to stable URLs or to an instruction page for the services that do not permit direct linking.
- A staff member views the document from the public interface for a final quality check.
- Access is limited to enrolled students through password protection or another authentication method.
- If necessary, duplicate working files are deleted from the server.
- At the end of the semester, staff members review the retain/release forms and appropriate documents are removed from view.
- If the items will be used again, a staff member reviews them for fair use.

Of course, this overview is necessarily general to allow for differences in electronic reserve systems. Workflow will vary according to whether or not electronic reserve processing is centralized to one unit or decentralized at various locations.

PERMISSIONS

While there are reasons to be wary, it is not necessary to seek permission for everything that will be digitized for electronic reserve. Determining fair use saves time, money, and recordkeeping. Permission is not needed if the work is in the public domain or if a license agreement covers the intended use. Otherwise permission should be sought.

The following questions should be considered when writing policy and procedures for the permissions process:

- Who will be responsible for procuring copyright permission?
- Must each faculty member prove permission?
- Will the library send the request?

- Will another campus unit, such as a bookstore or copy center, handle this process?
- How will payments be tracked and budgeted?

Permission must be received in writing from the copyright holder. The creator of the work is not necessarily the copyright holder. Copyrights may be transferred to publishers or assigned to someone else, but publishers usually hold the copyright.

Information about the copyright owner may be found in the copyright notice. This notice may accompany a statement about the use of materials, permissions contact information, or the transfer of rights. Note acknowledgments if the material was reproduced by permission and contact the acknowledged copyright holder. Permission to use figures, tables, maps, and so on may need to be requested separately if the source of the information is different than the copyright holder.

Where to Look for the Copyright Statement

Books

- Title page
- Page immediately following the title page
- Either side of the front or back cover
- First or last page of the main body of the work

Periodicals or Serials

- Title page
- Page immediately following the title page
- Either side of the front or back cover
- First or last page of the main body of the work
- As part of, or adjacent to, the masthead or on the page containing the masthead
- Adjacent to a prominent heading, appearing at or near the front of the issue, containing the title of the periodical and any combination of the volume, issue number, and date of the issue

Separate Contributions to Collective Works

- For a separate contribution reproduced on only one page, under the title or elsewhere on the same page
- For a separate contribution reproduced on more than one page

- Under a title appearing at or near the beginning of the contribution
- On the first page of the main body of the contribution
- Immediately following the end of the contribution
- On any of the pages where the contribution appears if the contribution consists of no more than 20 pages, the notice is reproduced prominently, and the application of the notice to the particular contribution is clear

Machine-Readable Copies

- With or near the title or at the end of the work, on visually perceptible printouts
- At sign-on
- On continuous display on the workstation
- Reproduced durably on a gummed or other label securely affixed to the copies or their containers

Audiovisual Works

- A notice embodied in the copies by a photo-mechanical or electronic process so that it ordinarily would appear whenever the work is performed in its entirety may be located
  - With or near the title
  - With the cast, credits, and similar information
  - At or immediately following the beginning of the work
  - At or immediately preceding the end of the work
- The notice on works lasting 60 seconds or less, such as untitled motion pictures or other audiovisual works, may be located
  - In all the locations specified above for longer motion pictures
  - If the notice is embodied electronically or photo-mechanically, on the leader of the film or tape immediately preceding the work
- For audiovisual works or motion pictures distributed to the public for private use, the locations include the above and, in addition, on the permanent housing or container

Pictorial, Graphic, and Sculptural Works

- For works embodied in two-dimensional copies, a notice may be affixed directly, durably, and permanently to

- The front or back of the copies
- Any backing, mounting, framing, or other material to which the copies are durably attached, so as to withstand normal use
- For works reproduced in three-dimensional copies, a notice may be affixed directly, durably, and permanently to
  - Any visible portion of the work
  - Any base, mounting, or framing or other material on which the copies are durably attached
- For works on which it is impractical to affix a notice to the copies directly or by means of a durable label, a notice is acceptable if it appears on a tag or durable label attached to the copy so that it will remain with it as it passes through commerce
- For works reproduced in copies consisting of sheet-like or strip material bearing multiple or continuous reproductions of the work, such as fabrics or wallpaper, the notice may be applied
  - To the reproduction itself
  - To the margin, selvage, or reverse side of the material at frequent and regular intervals
  - If the material contains neither a selvage nor reverse side, to tags or to labels attached to the copies and to any spools, reels, or containers housing them in such a way that the notice is visible in commerce (U.S. Copyright Office, 1999, *Circular 3*)

While use of a copyright notice was once required as a condition of copyright protection, it is now optional. Use of the notice is the responsibility of the copyright owner and does not require advance permission from, or registration with, the United States Copyright Office.

Many institutions routinely call the copyright holder first to find out if he or she will grant permission and at what fee. If permission is denied or the fee is prohibitive, they have saved valuable time. Another good idea is to confirm the contact name and address by phone or e-mail before sending the letter. The Association of American Publishers notes that, on average, permissions departments respond to requests within eight (8) weeks. Once you have sought permission, you must receive an affirmative written response–no response is not permission. You may also request that "RUSH" copyright permission be faxed to you in order to accommodate special situations.

Permission letters should include thorough descriptions of what, when, where, and how materials will be used. The letter should clearly state

- Title of the source
- Author of the work
- ISBN if available
- Page numbers

Indicate

- Name of the institution
- Course name and number
- Number of students enrolled in the class
- How access is restricted.

It is also important to ask specifically for permission to use the work in electronic format. Include a signature line for the copyright holder to indicate that permission has been granted.

AGENTS

When it has been determined that copyright permission must be requested, contact the copyright owner to find out if permission will be granted without a fee. Licensing agents may advertise as "one-stop shopping," but some copyright owners do not work with agents and want to deal directly with libraries. Agents usually charge a fee even if a publisher doesn't participate and the request is ultimately cancelled. Although agents mostly represent the interests of the copyright owners, they offer a necessary service. There often is little overlap between publishers who work directly with libraries and those who are represented by a licensing agent. Restrictive publisher policies often make this process more complicated than many administrators and faculty realize. One of the most time-consuming tasks in electronic reserve is tracking down the current copyright holder.

Royalty fees are determined through a variety of means for different publishers and agencies. There may be a copying fee, a fee based on number of students enrolled, a per-page fee, or any combination of those. Some publishers and electronic database vendors manage their own information access services that incorporate royalty payments.

The Copyright Clearance Center (CCC), Inc., was formed in 1978 to facilitate compliance with U. S. copyright law. The CCC provides licensing systems for the reproduction and distribution of over 1.75 million copyrighted materials in print and electronic formats throughout the world. Many libraries find that the online electronic course content service is a convenient way to obtain authorizations. Fees are based on copyright holder royalty fees plus a service charge. CANCOPY licenses through Access Copyright, the Canadian Copyright Licensing Agency, have provided a similar service in Canada. The International Federation of Reproduction Rights Organisations is a convenient place to learn more about licensing agents for foreign publishers that are not handled by these agencies.

PART TWO:
COPYRIGHT ISSUES
IN ELECTRONIC RESERVE

Chapter 4

An Overview of Copyright
and Fair Use

Copyright can be complicated and is often misunderstood. The basic principle of copyright is to protect a creator's rights of reproducing the work, distributing copies of the work, making derivative works, publicly performing or displaying the work. Copyright protection covers all literary and artistic works, encompassing diverse forms of creativity, such as writings (both fiction and nonfiction, including scientific and technical texts) and computer programs; databases that are original due to the selection or arrangement of their contents; musical works; audiovisual works; and works of fine art including drawings, paintings, and photographs (WIPO, p. 29).

Copyright is automatic for any "original work" that is "fixed in any tangible medium of expression" except for facts, slogans, titles, and

[Haworth co-indexing entry note]: "An Overview of Copyright and Fair Use." Driscoll, Lori. Co-published simultaneously in *Journal of Interlibrary Loan, Document Delivery & Information Supply* (The Haworth Information Press, an imprint of The Haworth Press, Inc.) Vol. 14, No. 1, 2003, pp. 35-43; and: *Electronic Reserve: A Manual and Guide for Library Staff Members* (Lori Driscoll) The Haworth Information Press, an imprint of The Haworth Press, Inc., 2003, pp. 35-43. Single or multiple copies of this article are available for a fee from The Haworth Document Delivery Service [1-800-HAWORTH, 9:00 a.m. - 5:00 p.m. (EST). E-mail address: docdelivery@haworthpress.com].

phrases. Works of the U.S. Government (but not necessarily state, local, or foreign governments) are usually not protected by copyright. A work is "fixed" in a "tangible medium of expression" when it is sufficiently permanent or stable to permit it to be perceived, reproduced, or otherwise communicated for a period of more than transitory duration. A work consisting of sounds, images, or both, that are being transmitted is "fixed" if a fixation of the work is being made simultaneously with its transmission (U.S. Copyright Law). Spontaneous speech or music that is not recorded is not protected by copyright.

The creator of the work owns the copyright but may transfer these rights to publishers or others. The exclusive rights provided by copyright are completely divisible. Copyright in a work is granted initially to the author or authors of the work, but the author may assign some or all of his or her rights to another (e.g., transferred to a publisher, if the work has appeared in a formal publication), who then becomes the owner of the rights assigned. In a work made for hire–that is a work prepared by an employee within the scope of employment or specially ordered or commissioned–the employer or other person for whom the work was prepared is considered the author (CENDI). Authors of a joint work jointly own the copyright.

The work is protected the moment it is created, regardless of whether there is a copyright notice or registration. The form of the copyright notice used for "visually perceptible" copies–that is, those that can be seen or read, either directly (such as books) or with the aid of a machine (such as films)–is different from the form used for phonorecords of sound recordings (such as compact discs or cassettes). The notice for visually perceptible copies contains all of the following:

1. *The symbol* © (the letter C in a circle), or the word "Copyright," or the abbreviation "Copr."
2. *The year of first publication*
3. *The name of the owner of copyright in the work*
   Example: © 1999 Jane Doe

Certain kinds of works, for example, musical, dramatic, and literary works may be fixed not in "copies" but by means of a recording. Copyright in a recording protects the particular series of sounds fixed in the recording against unauthorized reproduction, revision, and distribution. This copyright is distinct from copyright of the musical, literary, or dramatic work that may be recorded on the medium, for example, records (such as LPs and 45s), audiotapes, cassettes, or discs. The notice contains the following three elements appearing together on the recording:

1. *The symbol* Ⓟ (the letter P in a circle); and
2. *The year of first publication* of the sound recording; and
3. *The name of the owner of copyright.*
   Example: Ⓟ1999 X.Y.Z. Records, Inc.

(U.S. Copyright Office, June 1999, *Circular 3: Copyright Notice*)

This section has described what copyright *is*, but a historical discussion is necessary to provide insight into the current issues in copyright law.

A VERY BRIEF HISTORY OF COPYRIGHT LAW

Most discussions of copyright law refer to Title 17 of the U.S. Code and the 1976 Copyright Act; but laws concerning the publication of intellectual works have existed since the emergence of the printing press. The very foundation of copyright law in the United States is Article 1, Section 8, Clause 8 of the U.S. Constitution which states that "Congress shall have power . . . to promote the progress of science and useful arts, by securing for limited times to authors and inventors the exclusive right to their respective writings and discoveries." The first Copyright Act was passed in 1790, which gave authors the right to publish and reproduce their works for fourteen years, with an option to renew for another fourteen-year term. The intent of Congress was to facilitate the creation of work that advances science and art and to establish limits in order to provide public access to these works.

The Copyright Act was first revised in 1831 in order to extend the term of copyright to give American authors the same protection as Europeans (28 years with an option of another fourteen-year renewal period). It was revised again in 1870 to move the administration of copyright registrations to the Library of Congress. The 1909 revision widened the scope of protection to include all creative works (such as musical compositions, choreographed dances, and so on). The term of renewal was extended to twenty-eight years.

In 1976, the Copyright Act was significantly revised and preempted all existing copyright law. In order for the United States' law to be commensurate with international copyright law, the revision addressed the scope of the works covered, creative rights, term of protection, notice of copyright, infringement and fair use. This was the first time copyright law specifically addressed the issue of fair use.

Materials that are protected by current copyright law include the following:

I. Literary works

    a. Novels
    b. Poetry
    c. Articles in newspapers, magazines, and journals
    d. Brochures and catalogs
    e. Advertisements
    f. Compilations of facts like directories and databases

II. Artistic works

    a. Music
    b. Songs
    c. Sound recordings
    d. Operas
    e. Plays and skits
    f. Ballets, pantomimes, and choreographic works
    g. Motion pictures and other audiovisual works
    h. Drawings and cartoon strips
    i. Maps
    j. Architectural designs
    k. Photographs
    l. Paintings
    m. Statues and even stuffed animals (Radcliffe, 1999)

Copyright law does not provide protection for the following, regardless of the form in which they are described, explained, illustrated, or embodied:

I. Ideas
II. Procedures
III. Processes
IV. Methods of operation
V. Concepts
VI. Principles
VII. Discoveries

Computer software and documentation is protected by copyright, often with further protections offered through individual licensing agreements. However, nonprofit libraries are allowed to lend computer programs for nonprofit uses with a "Warning of Copyright Restrictions." Works on the Internet are treated like other textual, graphic, musical, and audiovisual formats; as soon as they are saved to a computer, they are considered "fixed." If they are not specifically public domain materials, they must pass a fair use test or permission must be obtained for their use.

Determining when a work is no longer protected by copyright was made more difficult due to other changes in the law occurring in 1988, 1992, and 1998. In 1989, the United States joined the Berne Convention for the Protection of Literary and Artistic Works to promote uniform international copyright protection; copyright notice no longer was required for copyright protection. This agreement protects the international market interests of creators in the United States. Despite this, there is no single international copyright law; copyright protection is dependent upon the laws of the particular country. An amendment in 1992 made copyright renewal automatic, significantly affecting the entry of works into the public domain. The term for copyright protection was extended again in 1998 with the Copyright Term Extension Act, later known as the Sonny Bono Term Extension Act. Congress has extended the term of copyright protection so frequently that it has, in effect, created an unlimited term of copyright protection. Although this has been challenged, the U.S. Supreme Court has upheld the constitutionality of these limits in the *Eldred v. Ashcroft* case.

DETERMINING COPYRIGHT PROTECTION

Date	Length of Copyright
Published before 1923	No longer protected by copyright
Published between 1923 and 1963 but copyright not renewed	No longer protected by copyright
Published before 1950 and copyright renewed before 1978	Copyright term is 95 years (28 plus renewal term of 67)
Published between 01/01/1950 and 12/31/1963	If not renewed, copyright expired after 28-year term; 95 years if renewed (28 plus 67)
Published between 01/01/1964 and 12/31/1977	67-year renewal term is automatic after 28 years, so copyright lasts 95 years
Copyright after 01/01/1978 or unpublished	Life of the last surviving author plus 70 years

Source: United States Copyright Office, *Circular 15a.* (2000)

WORKS IN PUBLIC DOMAIN

Works that are considered to be in the public domain are exempt from copyright protection. These materials may be used freely by anyone for any purpose. Public domain works include improvisational speeches or performances not fixed in a tangible form, works consisting of information that is common property with no original authorship (such as calendars, rules and measures), and works that have exceeded the period of copyright protection. Works in the public domain may be used by anyone, anywhere, anytime without permission, license, or royalty payment.

A U.S. Government work may enter the public domain if there is no other statutory basis to restrict its access. A work that is a privately created work and, with permission, is included in a U.S. Government work does not place the private work into the public domain. It is important to read the permissions and copyright notices on U.S. Government publications and web sites to determine whether or not the material is copyrighted. Publicly released, disclosed or disseminated information may be owned and protected by copyright and therefore may not be in the public domain (CENDI).

THE FAIR USE DOCTRINE

The fair use provision in the copyright law allows limited copying and distribution of works without the copyright owner's permission for purposes such as criticism, comment, teaching, scholarship and research. Additional provisions of the law also allow uses to further educational and library activities, such as archiving. Section 107 provides limitations on creators' copyrights and outlines acceptable purposes and factors to consider. Although the copyright law does allow for multiple copies for classroom use, it does not specify what or how much can be copied. When considering whether a particular case is fair use according to this section of the law, there are four factors to consider:

- *Purpose of the use.* Nonprofit educational use is more likely to be viewed as 'fair' than commercial use; multiple copies for classroom use is specifically mentioned in the statute.
- *Nature of the copyrighted work.* Numerous characteristics have been discussed in court cases, such as whether the work has been published, is out of print, is nonfiction rather than fiction, is in printed form rather than some other media, or is a workbook rather than a text. Some works are seen as more deserving of copyright protection than others.
- *Amount of the material used in relation to the copyrighted work.* A lesser quantity of and lesser substantiality (quality) of the material used are more likely to be fair use. Quantity as well as quality and importance should be considered: "No more was taken than necessary."

- *Effect of use on the potential market for or value of the copyrighted work.* A use for research and teaching is more likely to be fair than commercial use.

While fair use should be determined for the reproduction, distribution, display, and performance of materials in the electronic reserve system, permission from the copyright owner can expand the scope and range of materials included.

No courts have ruled on fair use in electronic reserve. Cases that relate to higher education involve for-profit uses, such as course packs and book publishing, not scholarship and teaching. Institutions have approached electronic reserve services in a variety of ways, with some interpretations of the Fair Use Doctrine being more restrictive than others. At one end of the spectrum are those libraries that attempt to receive permission for every item on reserve, and at the other end are those libraries who either view all reserve services in the purview of fair use or who place the responsibility for seeking permission on faculty.

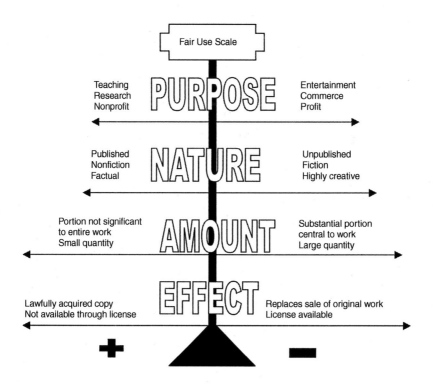

TEACH ACT

New laws have clarified the use of materials in a distance-learning venue, supporting exceptions to copyrights for educational purposes. The Technology Education and Copyright Harmonization (TEACH) Act revises Section 110(2) of the Copyright Act, allowing accredited, nonprofit educational institutions to use copyrighted materials in distance education without obtaining permission and without paying copyright fees. This law expands the scope of materials (display and performance of nearly all types of works), allows for the delivery of content to any location, permits the retention of archival copies on servers, and provides some conventions for converting analog to digital format in order to facilitate transmission. These benefits are balanced with conditions to create and disseminate copyright policies and resources, to apply technology to restrict access to enrolled students, and to prevent further distribution.

To comply with this copyright exemption, the TEACH Act requires

- An accredited nonprofit educational institution,
- A copyright compliance policy,
- Educational materials on copyright;

that the work

- Is not readily available in digital format,
- Is lawfully obtained,
- Is an integral part of class and systematic mediated instructional activities;

and that technological control must be in place in order to

- Limit access to students enrolled in course,
- Control further distribution,
- Display a warning notice to students.

Because the use of materials is framed within the context of "mediated instructional activities," it remains uncertain whether or not reserves and other outside reading may be scanned under this provision. This introduction of technological controls over the use of electronic information resources brings libraries into a new model of access.

Libraries are acquiring more and more materials that are already in digital form: electronic journals, e-books and full-text article databases. These materials are not purchased like printed materials but are licensed for use by the library from the content providers. A license agreement is the contract between the library and the copyright owner for the use of these materials. Copies of works obtained through licensing are subject to the additional terms of the agreement. Through such agreements, libraries have the opportunity to specify permission for electronic course reserve use.

Although copyright is often misunderstood, there are basic principles to guide interpretation for electronic reserve. Copyright law primarily exists to balance a creator's right to benefit from the reproduction of a work with the public's right to advance knowledge and expression. Electronic reserve use of materials is guided by the Fair Use Doctrine that equally weighs purpose of use, nature of the copyrighted work, amount and substantiality of material from original work, and the effect of use on the value of the protected work. The next chapter discusses the implications of Fair Use on electronic reserve services further.

Chapter 5

Fair Use for Electronic Reserve

Course reserve has always been a supplemental source of information for students. The materials placed on reserve are not intended to replace textbooks but to provide wider access to frequently used materials. Electronic reserve materials are varied. Some items may already be digitized, while others must be converted from analog to digital format. Some documents may be in the public domain, while authors or publishers hold the rights to others. The most critical consideration for materials to be included in course reserves, whether printed or electronic, is the determination of fair use. However, with permission or licensing, the scope and range of materials to be included are only limited by the copyright owners. The technology exists to restrict access to electronic reserve items even more stringently than printed course reserve materials in libraries. But there is considerable debate as to the applicability of printed guidelines for fair use of electronic materials. Copyright holders are concerned that more copies of a work are made in electronic systems, and there is no degradation of quality in the copies–all "copies" are essentially "masters."

GUIDELINES AND POLICY STATEMENTS

At the same time copyright law changed in 1976, groups representing educational institutions and the publishing industry adopted the "Agreement on Guidelines for Classroom Copying in Not-for-Profit Educational

[Haworth co-indexing entry note]: "Fair Use for Electronic Reserve." Driscoll, Lori. Co-published simultaneously in *Journal of Interlibrary Loan, Document Delivery & Information Supply* (The Haworth Information Press, an imprint of The Haworth Press, Inc.) Vol. 14, No. 1, 2003, pp. 45-52; and: *Electronic Reserve: A Manual and Guide for Library Staff Members* (Lori Driscoll) The Haworth Information Press, an imprint of The Haworth Press, Inc., 2003, pp. 45-52. Single or multiple copies of this article are available for a fee from The Haworth Document Delivery Service [1-800-HAWORTH, 9:00 a.m. - 5:00 p.m. (EST). E-mail address: docdelivery@haworthpress.com].

Institutions with Respect to Books and Periodicals" to provide minimum standards for educational fair use (http://www.musiclibraryassoc.org/ Copyright/guidebks.htm). The classroom copying guidelines emphasize brevity, spontaneity, cumulative effects, and copyright notice. The Supreme Court has cited these with approval for nonprofit educational institutions but the guidelines have not been specifically tried in copyright cases. These guidelines were not useful to the unique requirements of higher education or libraries, so clearer guidelines were necessary.

ALA MODEL POLICY

The American Library Association developed the "Model Policy Concerning College and University Photocopying for Classroom, Research and Library Reserve Use" in 1982 to address fair use rights for teaching, research, and library services <http://www.cni.org/docs/ infopols/ALA.html-mpup>. Intended as a guide for library policy-making, it outlines situations in which unrestricted photocopying is permissible, those permissible as fair use, and those requiring permission from the copyright owner. This document continues to serve as the basis for most library reserve service decisions, but it has been removed from the ALA web site. The guidelines have generally been considered safe because they have never been challenged in court.

In respect to reserve collections, the guidelines state that requests should meet the following guidelines:

1. The amount of material should be reasonable in relation to the total amount of material assigned for one term of a course, taking into account the nature of the course, its subject matter, and level. (*Brevity*)
2. The number of copies should be reasonable in light of the number of students enrolled, the difficulty and timing of assignments, and the number of other courses that may assign the same material. (*Spontaneity*)
3. The material should contain a notice of copyright. (*Copyright notice*)
4. The effect of photocopying the material should not be detrimental to the market for the work, that is, generally, the library should own at least one copy of the work. (*Cumulative effects*)

CONFU

This Model Policy served the library community for over a decade, until advances in technology required specific guidelines for distance education and electronic reserves. The Conference on Fair Use (CONFU) brought together a diverse group of interested parties to draft guidelines addressing fair use in distance education, interlibrary loan, and electronic reserves. Competing interests kept the guidelines from being widely supported, and they have not been endorsed consistently by major library organizations. (For the full report, refer to http://www. uspto.gov/web/offices/dcom/lia/confu/confurep.htm.) The Fair-Use Guidelines for Electronic Reserve Systems (Crews, 1999) that are based on the CONFU guidelines are available at http://www.copyright.iupui. edu/fu_ereserve_guide.htm. Because these are guidelines for fair use, they do not apply to works in the public domain or items for which permission has been granted through a release or license agreement. Although these guidelines were never agreed upon, they are reproduced here for later discussion:

Scope of material

1. In accordance with fair use (Section 107 of the U.S. Copyright Act), electronic reserve systems may include copyrighted materials at the request of a course instructor.
2. Electronic reserve systems may include short items (such as an article from a journal, a chapter from a book or conference proceedings, or a poem from a collected work) or excerpts from longer items. "Longer items" may include articles, chapters, poems, and other works that are of such length as to constitute a substantial portion of a book, journal, or other work of which they may be a part. "Short items" may include articles, chapters, poems, and other works of a customary length and structure as to be a small part of a book, journal, or other work, even if that work may be marketed individually.
3. Electronic reserve systems should not include any material unless the instructor, the library, or another unit of the educational institution possesses a lawfully obtained copy.
4. The total amount of material included in electronic reserve systems for a specific course as a matter of fair use should be a small proportion of the total assigned reading for a particular course.

Notices and Attributions

1. On a preliminary or introductory screen, electronic reserve systems should display a notice, consistent with the notice described in Section 108(f)(1) of the Copyright Act. The notice should include additional language cautioning against further electronic distribution of the digital work.

2. If a notice of copyright appears on the copy of a work that is included in an electronic reserve system, the following statement shall appear at some place where users will likely see it in connection with access to the particular work: "The work from which this copy is made includes this notice: [restate the elements of the statutory copyright notice: e.g., Copyright 1996, XXX Corp.]."

3. Materials included in electronic reserve systems should include appropriate citations or attributions to their sources.

Access and Use

1. Electronic reserve systems should be structured to limit access to students registered in the course for which the items have been placed on reserve, and to instructors and staff members responsible for the course or the electronic system.

2. The appropriate methods for limiting access will depend on available technology. Solely to suggest and not to prescribe options for implementation, possible methods for limiting access may include one or more of the following or other appropriate methods:
   a. individual password controls or verification of a student's registration status;
   b. password system for each class;
   c. retrieval of works by course number or instructor name, but not by author or title of the work;
   d. access limited to workstations that are ordinarily used by, or are accessible to, only enrolled students or appropriate staff members or faculty.

3. Students should not be charged specifically or directly for access to electronic reserve systems.

Storage and Reuse

1. Permission from the copyright holder is required if the item is to be reused in a subsequent academic term for the same course offered by the same instructor, or if the item is a standard assigned or optional reading for an individual course taught in multiple sections by many instructors.

2. Material may be retained in electronic form while permission is being sought or until the next academic term in which the material might be used, but in no event for more than three calendar years, including the year in which the materials are last used.

3. Short-term access to materials included on electronic reserve systems in previous academic terms may be provided to students who have not completed the course.

OTHER GUIDELINES

Guidelines proposed by publishers, most often focus on access, substantiality, spontaneity, attribution, and notice of copyright (AAP). Access can be limited to library workstations, by technologically blocking download of the material or assigning passwords, authenticating by IP, limiting access to students enrolled but not the general public, and limiting search parameters by only indexing items by class name rather than item title or author. This ensures that bibliographic access is no greater than that available for other books and journals in the collection.

Substantiality is addressed by minimizing the amount of material used. Spontaneity is demonstrated with the decision to use the work coinciding with the maximum teaching effectiveness when there is no time to receive permission to use it, or simply a one-time use.

Attribution to the creator of the work is accomplished by providing the complete citation information. It is also important that the content of the material not be modified. Copyright warnings should accompany the items, along with an official statement of copyright from the publisher. This statement usually contains the copyright designation, copyright holder's name, and the date of publication. The publisher-supplied copyright statement should be used unless the publisher does not provide one. Since many users may not consider electronic distribution "copying," the AAP encourages the inclusion of a statement specifically prohibiting further distribution.

FAIR USE IN THE ELECTRONIC AGE

A statement developed by the American Association of Law Libraries, American Library Association, Association of Academic Health Sciences Library Directors, Association of Research Libraries, Medical Library Association, and Special Library Association is "Fair Use in the Electronic Age: Serving the Public Interest." The Art Libraries Society of North America has also endorsed this document. The statement promotes the fair use provision as a means to balance the rights of the public to promote the dissemination of knowledge while ensuring copyright owners protection for their creative works and economic investments. Also stated, "The preservation and continuation of these balanced rights in an electronic environment as well as in traditional formats are essential to the free flow of information and to the development of an information infrastructure that serves the public interest." More information is becoming available in electronic format only. The "Fair Use in the Electronic Age" document asserts that nonprofit libraries should be able to provide copyrighted materials as part of electronic reserve room service without infringing copyright.

CURRENT PRACTICES

Institutions on the cutting edge have had relatively long-standing policies and procedures regarding electronic reserve services. Some range from a very conservative approach to determining fair use to those with a very broad interpretation. Since 1997, it has been the policy of the University of Wisconsin Libraries that materials in their collections are purchased with the understanding that there will be multiple uses of a limited number of copies, and journal subscription prices reflect this support of multiple academic users. In this interpretation, the electronic reserve system facilitates the making of multiple copies for classroom use by students and is fair use of these materials (Electronic Reserves Guide, Murphy Library, University of Wisconsin–La Crosse, http://www.uwlax.edu/murphylibrary/departments/eresguide.html).

The Copyright Management Center at Indiana University Purdue University at Indianapolis provides faculty with guidelines regarding fair use in electronic reserves. The purpose of the use must be to serve the needs of specified educational programs, at the request of the instructor, with limited access to materials in order to deter unauthorized access beyond students enrolled in the course. Students cannot be charged for access and the university cannot benefit monetarily from the use of the material. The nature of the materials placed on reserve must be directly related to the educational objectives of a specific course, and only relevant portions may be used. The amount is limited to brief works or brief excerpts from longer works. To ensure that the effect of use on the market for the original is fair, repeat use of the same material by the same instructor for the same course requires permission; the materials must originate from a lawfully obtained copy owned by the instructor or institution. Materials require a citation of the original source and a copyright notice. Access to materials is limited to enrolled students. The materials cannot replace those available for purchase such as a text, workbook, or course pack. For the complete guidelines, refer to the Electronic Reserves web page at http://www.copyright.iupui.edu/ereserves.htm.

LICENSING PROJECTS

Libraries are increasingly licensing electronic resources for use by our faculty and students. Over the past decade, the percentage of the materials budget allocated to electronic resources has quadrupled in research libraries (ARL, 2002). Access to these resources usually requires some means of user authentication. When libraries have the opportunity to sign standard license agreements that allow for the use of resources in electronic reserve, the current compliance conundrum may be solved. Projects like ARTstor and JSTOR may provide collaborative opportunities for institutions to build digital collections that may be licensed for nominal fees.

- ARTstor is a project of the Mellon Foundation to develop, "store," and distribute electronically digital images and related scholarly materials for the study of art, architecture, and other fields in the humanities . . . ARTstor's mission is to provide access to high-quality digital images and other relevant materials for teachers, students, and scholars at educational and cultural institutions . . . ARTstor also aims to reduce costs for participating institutions by eliminating the need for each entity or institution to create its own core archive . . . In working with content providers, the Foundation and ARTstor have obtained perpetual, nonexclusive rights to aggregate such materials, to incorporate them into the repository, and distribute them electronically for noncommercial educational and scholarly purposes . . . In addition to serving the needs of teachers and scholars, one goal of these projects is to support the mission of institutions that seek to expand access to their own holdings for academic audiences without incurring the financial and administrative burdens of distribution (Rudenstine & Shulman, 2003).
- JSTOR's mission is to help the scholarly community take advantage of advances in information technologies, taking into account the sometimes conflicting needs of libraries, publishers, and scholars. JSTOR's relevant goals include building a reliable and comprehensive archive of important scholarly journal literature, dramatically improving access to these journals, and reducing long-term capital and operating costs of libraries associated with the storage and care of journal collections (JSTOR, 2002).

Other approaches have also been undertaken to make public domain materials readily available, such as Project Gutenberg. Most recently, the Creative Commons released two projects: the Licensing Project to allow creators to stipulate conditions for free use, and Founders' Copyright to make content available for 14 years as our founding fathers originally intended.

There are legitimate reasons to be concerned about copyright infringement. If an organization is found in violation, the Court can take any equipment used for the infringement. It can also order payment to the copyright owner the value of the loss, statutory damages of $30,000, and attorney fees. However, when acting within the bounds of fair use and taking reasonable measures to protect the interests of copyright owners, nonprofit educational institutions are unlikely to infringe copyright. Most institutions feel that using some set of guidelines will at least show "good faith." Ochoa (2002) suggests that libraries may take comfort in knowing that "content owners almost always send a cease-and-desist letter before taking legal action" (p. 2). This is supported by a report from the General Accounting Office (2001) that found that less than 0.05% (58) of all intellectual property lawsuits filed since 1985 (for all forms of intellectual property: patents, trademarks, and copyrights) listed a state entity as the defendant.

Staff members want common sense policies and procedures that are easy to adopt. The second half of this book will attempt to provide sound advice for such policies and procedures based on the current status of copyright law.

Chapter 6

Frequently Asked Questions

FROM STUDENTS

What is electronic course reserve?

Electronic course reserve is a counterpart to the traditional Library Reserve collection, where professors make supplementary course materials available to students. Students can access items 24 hours a day, 7 days a week, from anywhere with an Internet connection and a web browser.

Are all course readings available electronically?

Only course materials that have been placed on electronic reserve by your professor will be available.

How do I access the materials for my course?

Connect through the Library home page to the Electronic Course Reserve System. You may search for reserve material by the name of the course, department, or professor.

[Haworth co-indexing entry note]: "Frequently Asked Questions." Driscoll, Lori. Co-published simultaneously in *Journal of Interlibrary Loan, Document Delivery & Information Supply* (The Haworth Information Press, an imprint of The Haworth Press, Inc.) Vol. 14, No. 1, 2003, pp. 53-59; and: *Electronic Reserve: A Manual and Guide for Library Staff Members* (Lori Driscoll) The Haworth Information Press, an imprint of The Haworth Press, Inc., 2003, pp. 53-59. Single or multiple copies of this article are available for a fee from The Haworth Document Delivery Service [1-800-HAWORTH, 9:00 a.m. - 5:00 p.m. (EST). E-mail address: docdelivery@haworthpress.com].

10.1300/J110v14n01_06

What kind of hardware and software will I need to view electronic reserve material?

You will need a computer with Internet access. Most electronic reserve items will be in Portable Document Format (PDF). In PDF, the document looks like the original. The PDF reader is free. It is available for download from http://www.adobe.com/products/acrobat/.

After my professor submits material to the Library, when will it appear on reserve?

During the beginning of a school term, we may require up to 5 business days to completely process electronic reserve items. If you check the electronic reserve system and don't find an item you expect to see, please contact us.

How can I increase the print size on the screen if it is too small to read?

In Adobe Acrobat, click on the magnifying glass icon located on the tool bar immediately above the text. Then place your cursor over the specific area you want to enlarge and click again.

Why do files take so long to download?

The download time depends on the file size and your Internet connection. Larger files take longer to download. If you are using a modem and phone line, it will take longer than if you are using a cable modem or DSL connection.

Why do I need a password to view some reserve items?

In order to comply with United States Copyright Law, access to copyrighted items must be restricted to faculty and students. The password confirms that you are enrolled in the class for which the items were placed on reserve.

FROM FACULTY

How do I submit my materials? Can a graduate assistant place items on reserve for me?

Items may be submitted at the Reserve Desk or electronically through the form on the Library's home page. You must sign the *Instructor Cer-*

tification of Copyright Compliance form, but you may send the signed form and materials through a proxy.

Why do I still have to bring in a photocopy? Can't you just scan from the original?

Some locations can scan only letter-sized sheets not bound materials. It also expedites processing time so that your materials are available to students sooner.

How long will my materials remain on the Electronic Reserve System?

Six weeks before the end of a semester, the Library will send a Retain or Release form for all items you have placed on electronic reserve. Routine release of these items begins on the last day of each semester. You may be required to resubmit certification of copyright compliance.

Will everything be converted to electronic reserve?

No. Traditional, physical course reserve will remain a service offered by the Library, both for copyright reasons and technological limitations. The following examples are not acceptable for electronic reserve:

- Whole books
- Any material that cannot be reduced to letter-size
- Any non-print media item that is not digitized.

Will there be physical copies of electronic reserve items as backup?

Whenever possible, items will be placed on electronic reserve. Other items will be on traditional reserve, but there will not be duplication between the two systems.

I'm in a rush! What can I do to speed the processing of my list?

1. Submit digitized files for your course reserve materials. Files in PDF, MS Word, or PowerPoint formats can be processed more quickly than paper documents that have to be scanned.
2. Provide a timeline when materials are needed to help us prioritize the processing workload.

3. Completely fill out your Request Form. If your list includes photocopies of published material, provide a clean photocopy with a full source citation, including photocopies of the title page and copyright page.
4. Use materials that clearly fall under standards of fair use. If your selections of photocopied materials meet the fair use standards, the library will not need to verify or request permission from the publishers.
5. If the use of your materials cannot be considered fair use, obtain permission in advance from the publisher or copyright holder to use the materials specifically for electronic course reserve. Give the library a copy of the documentation to file with the processed materials.

Is there a limit to the number of chapters per book that can be submitted to electronic reserve?

Only one chapter of a book may be placed on electronic reserve while permission is sought. The copyright owner will indicate the acceptable limit.

What is the verso title page and why do I need to submit it for every article I'm placing on electronic reserve?

The verso is the left-hand or backside page of a bound work; the copyright statement and publishers' information is usually printed on the verso of the title page. In order to comply with copyright guidelines, the reserve staff members must include the publisher's copyright statement with each article.

A student gave me permission for me to use his paper for future classes. I have included the paper with my print course reserves, but I would now like to place it on electronic reserve. Can the student's paper be scanned?

It depends on the extent of permissions given; but, in general, electronic distribution must be treated separately from print distribution.

Am I responsible for obtaining copyright permission? Who pays the royalty fees?

When using the Library's electronic reserve system, the library will seek copyright permissions and pay reasonable fees. Should the fees for an article for one semester's use exceed $100, we will contact you to discuss how to share the cost or to suggest alternatives.

Do I need written permission from every author in a multi-author paper for it to be placed on electronic reserve?

It depends on who owns the copyright, but all authors potentially hold those rights equally.

Doesn't electronic reserve violate copyright?

Copyright is a very complex topic and the Library has made a great effort to create informational materials about copyright law. Electronic course reserve materials are generally subject to the same standard for determining "fair use" as traditional course reserve materials.

Isn't any use of copyrighted material for educational purposes a fair use?

The purpose of the use is only one of the four factors courts consider. Case law indicates that no one factor is more important than any other. So the fact that your use is educational is just one thing the court might look at if a copyright holder decided to sue you for damages.

Copyright doesn't apply to works that are out of print, does it?

Although this is a common misconception, copyright protection lasts until a specified time period after the death of the author, or in the case of corporate authorship, a specified time after the work is created. Whether the item is in or out of print has no bearing on whether it's protected. It may be easier to receive permission to digitize out of print materials, however.

What is "public domain"?

Works in the public domain are not protected by copyright and may be used or copied freely. All copyrighted works eventually enter the public domain when the copyright protection expires. Some documents are always public domain no matter when or who created them.

Can I legally copy a work I bought without infringing the copyright?

The purchaser of a work owns only that particular copy of the work, not the copyright. You cannot copy the purchased work, in whole or in part, without the copyright owner's permission unless such copying constitutes "fair use."

Can I go ahead and use the item when I have requested permission on several occasions and haven't received a response?

Do not assume that you have permission to use the material if you haven't received a response to your request. You may wish to follow up through another channel of communication.

What can I do if course material has been ordered for a class but is late in arriving at the bookstore?

Publishers vary on their policies, but you may be able to obtain permission from the copyright owner to photocopy a portion of the material until the book arrives. Contact the copyright owner for the preferred procedure.

Can I use an article I wrote for a publication?

It depends on your contract with the publisher. Have you transferred copyright to that company or do you own the rights?

How do I handle copyright permission for a work containing a photograph or illustration with a copyright owner different from that of the work itself?

The publisher of the original material has received permission from the photographer or illustrator to include the image in the work but may or may not have the right to grant reproduction rights to others. In some cases, licensing agents act on behalf of the photographer or illustrator, but you may need to make a separate request for permission to copy the photograph or illustration.

Realistically, how likely is it that I will be held personally responsible for copyright infringement? Would anyone actually sue me?

Civil and criminal penalties may be imposed for copyright infringement. Civil judgments can include an award of monetary damages (statutory damages, or actual damages, including the infringer's profits), an award of attorney's fees, injunctive relief against future infringement, and the impounding and destruction of infringing copies. In some circumstances educators are not required to pay statutory damages; nonetheless, they may be responsible for paying the copyright owner actual damages caused by their infringement, as well as attorney's fees. However, there has not been a court case specifically addressing the use of material in electronic reserve.

What is "Sovereign Immunity"? How can I reduce my risk for litigation?

Sovereign Immunity is based on the 11th Amendment to the U.S. Constitution. In this context, sovereign immunity protects government and state entities, including public universities, from copyright litigation. While the copyright code includes a statement that employees are not immune under the 11th Amendment, the Supreme Court asserted in *College Savings Bank v. Florida* that the 11th Amendment supercedes federal statutes (Bodi, 2003). The best practice is to follow the policies and procedures that we have developed in consultation with our legal counsel. Private colleges and universities do not usually have Sovereign Immunity.

Are there alternatives to electronic course reserve?

Course software can be used to provide access to supplementary materials through the course web site. Course packs generated at a copy shop can also provide an alternative for many materials that require permission for use.

Appendix

Sample Policies, Forms, and Checklists

This sample policy document attempts to consolidate all policy statements and guidelines contained within this work. At this fictitious institution, the library secures copyright permissions on behalf of the faculty. Institutions that require faculty to perform this task can adapt this policy to fit those requirements upfront. Institutions that have specific guidelines for policy documents can also adapt this sample policy to fit that specific format.

University Library Electronic Reserve Policy

The University Library provides an electronic course reserve service to support teaching activities at the University. These guidelines regulate the submission and handling of electronic course reserve materials. The University Library's Electronic Course Reserve Unit must comply with United States Copyright Law. The Library exercises the right to determine conditions of use and may refuse materials for reserve for legal or other reasons. Faculty and students are responsible for complying with copyright law. More information about copyright is available on the University Library's Copyright page at http://www.library.university.edu/copyright.html.

Any faculty member may place materials on electronic course reserve. Items are indexed in the electronic reserves system by faculty member name and course number. Digitized text, image, audio, and video materials may be considered. Class notes, exams, syllabi, homework, student papers, copies of articles, and other materials are scanned so that the text

[Haworth co-indexing entry note]: "Appendix. Sample Policies, Forms, and Checklists." Driscoll, Lori. Co-published simultaneously in *Journal of Interlibrary Loan, Document Delivery & Information Supply* (The Haworth Information Press, an imprint of The Haworth Press, Inc.) Vol. 14, No. 1, 2003, pp. 61-86; and: *Electronic Reserve: A Manual and Guide for Library Staff Members* (Lori Driscoll) The Haworth Information Press, an imprint of The Haworth Press, Inc., 2003, pp. 61-86. Single or multiple copies of this article are available for a fee from The Haworth Document Delivery Service [1-800-HAWORTH, 9:00 a.m. - 5:00 p.m. (EST). E-mail address: docdelivery@haworth press.com].

http://www.haworthpress.com/store/product.asp?sku=J110
© 2003 by The Haworth Press, Inc. All rights reserved.
10.1300/J110v14n01_07

is available to students online. If the Library has electronic access to the item, an electronic link will be provided from the reserve record. Access to electronic reserve materials is limited to current University students and faculty and is authenticated through IP address or proxy server.

Only materials that are in compliance with copyright law may be placed on electronic course reserve. A signed Copyright Release form must accompany the submission of works produced by students or faculty, and every author must sign. The Library will secure copyright permission for other materials that are scanned for electronic reserve and will pay any associated fees. If permission is not granted or the copyright royalty fee is prohibitively high, the Library will notify the faculty member and the materials will not be available for electronic course reserve. All efforts will be made to include items in electronic reserves, but if they are not eligible, print course reserves may be an alternative.

Materials submitted must contain the copyright statement from the source publication. Even if a copyright statement was not published with the material, the work may be copyrighted. The Library will add a copyright notice to the electronic document:

WARNING CONCERNING COPYRIGHT RESTRICTIONS

The copyright law of the United States (Title 17, United States Code) governs the making of photocopies or other reproductions of copyrighted material. Under certain conditions specified in the law, libraries and archives are authorized to furnish a photocopy or other reproduction. One of these specific conditions is that the photocopy or reproduction is not to be 'used for any purpose other than private study, scholarship, or research.' If a user makes a request for, or later uses, a photocopy or reproduction for purposes in excess of 'fair use,' that user may be liable for copyright infringement. These materials are made available for the educational purposes of students enrolled at [name of institution]. No further reproduction, transmission, or electronic distribution of this material is permitted.

Faculty may submit either electronic files or print copies that the Library will convert to formats that can be viewed or heard from freely available application tools such as Adobe Acrobat Reader and Real Player. Most materials will be processed for electronic reserves within five (5) business days. However, more time may be necessary for requests submitted on or after the first day of class or lacking information or materials. To ensure that readings will be on reserve for the first day of class for the next semester, please allow 6-8 weeks for copyright clearance. Source materials will be returned through campus mail as soon as electronic documents have been created. Faculty should not expect materials to be processed and available at the time of submission. At the end of each semester, all materials on electronic course reserve must be renewed for the next semester including copyright clearance, or the materials will be released and made inaccessible.

Six weeks before the end of the semester faculty will receive a Renew/Release form regarding the items on electronic reserve. Materials to be renewed or released for the next term should be indicated. After receipt of the form, the Library will remove the materials to be released from reserve within five (5) days of the end of the semester.

Concise guidelines for staff members to use as a quick reference are also useful. The University of Texas and others have developed fair use "Rule of Thumb" for use by reserve unit staff members (see http://www.utsystem.edu/ogc/intellectualproperty/copypol2. htm-reserve).

Rule of Thumb

Situations that are not covered by these rules are referred to the reserve coordinator:

1. Limit reserve materials to

   - Single articles or chapters; several charts, graphs or illustrations; or other small parts of a work
   - A small part of the materials required for the course
   - Copies of materials that a faculty member or the library already legally owns (i.e., by purchase, license, fair use, interlibrary loan, etc.).

2. Include

   - Any copyright notice from the original
   - Appropriate citations and attributions to the source
   - A library copyright warning notice.

3. Limit access to students enrolled in the class and administrative staff members as needed; terminate access at the end of the semester.
4. Obtain permission for materials that will be used repeatedly by the same instructor for the same class.

General Guidelines of Electronic Course Reserve

All items for course reserve must

1. Be legible
2. Include the complete citation on the first page
3. Include the publisher's copyright statement.

We can place the following materials on electronic reserve

1. Student- or professor-generated materials with signed permission form
2. Items published prior to 1923
3. Other items determined to be in the public domain
4. Links to e-books or e-journals in our databases
5. A single chapter that has not been used for this course or professor from a book that is lawfully obtained (owned by professor or library or received via interlibrary loan)
6. A single article that has not been used for this course or professor from a journal that is lawfully obtained (owned by professor or library or received via interlibrary loan)
7. Any item for which permission from the copyright holder has been granted.

We must FIRST receive permission to use

1. Unpublished works
2. Consumables (workbooks, exercises, standardized tests and test booklets, answer sheets, etc.)
3. Anything from a source that has already been used by the same professor for the same course
4. Multiple articles from the same issue of a journal (one may be selected until permission is received for the remainder) for the same course and professor
5. Multiple chapters from a book (one may be selected until permission is received for the remainder) for the same course and professor
6. Multiple excerpts from an anthology or other collective work (one may be selected until original sources may be located and utilized) for the same course and professor.

Guidelines for Instructors

Prepare and submit library forms listing all items to be placed on electronic reserve. Please follow all instructions detailed on the list. Many copyrighted articles and other items have been purchased or licensed by the Library in full text through electronic journals, e-books, or article databases. Faculty are encouraged to identify and assign these whenever possible. The Library will provide links or access information to these items. For other copyrighted materials, the Library will seek permission from the copyright owner. If permission is denied, the Library cannot place the item on electronic reserve. Excessive fees charged by copyright holders may also prohibit making certain materials available. In these instances, the Library will inform the professor.

Meet advertised deadlines for submission in order to ensure that items will be available by the first day of class. Items received after the deadline will be processed as soon as possible in the order received. Due to processing time, allow at least five days before material is needed for student use. Do not assume that items will be available immediately upon delivery. When possible, deliver all items with the list to ensure maximum processing speed. Photocopies should be neat and single-sided on 8.5″ × 11″ paper. Provide the highest-quality copy for best results. Photocopies of journal articles or single book chapters must have the complete citation imprinted or clearly written on the item and include a photocopy of the publisher's copyright statement. Items submitted in electronic format will save processing time. The Library will add a notice of copyright to photocopies of copyrighted materials submitted for electronic reserve.

Request to Place Items on Electronic Reserve

University Library Electronic Reserves Office
(321) 555-1234 or e-mail: reserves@library.university.edu

Semester/Year: Fall   Spring   Summer A/B/C   200_

Course Name & Number: _____

Section Number: _____

Professor Name: _____

Department: _____

Campus Mailing Address: _____

Office Phone Number: _____

E-mail: _____

Provide the complete citation information below to expedite process-ing. Please place an "X" next to the citation if you have used an item for electronic reserve before so that the permissions process may be initi-ated.

Source Title (Book/Journal)   Author   Chapter/Article Title   Pages

_____

Instructor Certification of Copyright Compliance

Please mark as appropriate and sign the certification statement below.

____ I give permission to put works for which I own the copyright on electronic reserve until further notice.

____ I have secured permission from a student whose work I request to place on electronic reserve. The signed permission statement is below.

____ I have secured the permission of the copyright holders to place their copyrighted work on electronic reserve. Copies of such permission letters are attached.

____ I am requesting that the Library secure permission from the copyright owner. I understand there may be a delay in the processing of submitted materials during this time. (If the Library cannot obtain a copyright release or if the copyright royalty is excessively high, the Library will immediately notify the instructor.)

Certification Statement

I certify that I am in compliance with University Library Electronic Reserve Policy and copyright law.

Instructor Name: _____ Course Number: _____

Instructor Signature: _____ Date: _____

As a University student, I _____ give permission to put works for which I own the copyright on electronic reserve until further notice.

Student signature _____ Date: _____

Checklists can help public service staff members obtain all the necessary documentation when first accepting materials that will be forwarded to Reserve Coordinators.

Public Service Desk Checklist

Refer faculty to the Reserves Coordinator. If the Reserves Coordinator is not available, accept the materials after completing this checklist for each item:

____ The copy is legible.

____ The item has the complete citation on the front page.

    ____ Author

    ____ Title (of excerpt)

    ____ Title (of source, if applicable)

    ____ Year of copyright

    ____ Volume/number/issue/chapter

    ____ Page numbers

____ Citation matches the material.

____ Publisher's copyright statement is also included.

____ There is a signed permission form for a student's or professor's unpublished material.

____ Professor has completed the Course Reserve form for this material.

____ Record the name of the person delivering the materials if not the faculty member:

_____

Date: Your Name:

When reserve units are decentralized, e.g., each branch has its own reserve coordinator, with a central Permissions Coordinator for copyright clearance, the following checklist can streamline the process that routes items to that individual.

Reserve Coordinator Checklist

___ The copy is legible.
___ The item has the complete citation on the front page.
    ___ Author
    ___ Title (of excerpt)
    ___ Title (of source, if applicable)
    ___ Year of copyright
    ___ Volume/number/issue/chapter
    ___ Page numbers
___ Citation matches the material.
___ Publisher's copyright statement is also included.
___ There is a signed permission form for a student's or professor's unpublished material.
___ Professor has completed the Course Reserve form for this material.
___ No part of any consumables (workbooks, exercises, standardized tests and test booklets, answer sheets, etc.) may be placed on electronic reserve. Ask faculty if they want us to place on paper reserve. Forward to Permissions Coordinator.
___ Requests for unpublished works should be forwarded to Permissions Coordinator for immediate review.
___ Determine ownership and electronic availability of item by searching catalog.
___ Link directly to electronic item, if available.
___ If work was published before 1923, any quantity may be used and review may stop here.
___ If the copy is not from a lawfully obtained source (owned by the library or professor or received via interlibrary loan), forward to Permissions Coordinator for immediate review.
___ There is no more than one chapter from the same book, one article from the same issue of a journal, or one excerpt from a collective work or anthology.
    ___ Search for original sources of excerpts from an anthology.
___ The journal, book, or anthology has not been used previously or concurrently for this course. If used more than once, forward to Permissions Coordinator for immediate review.
    ___ If we do not own the item, forward purchase request to acquisitions.

Reserve Workflow Chart

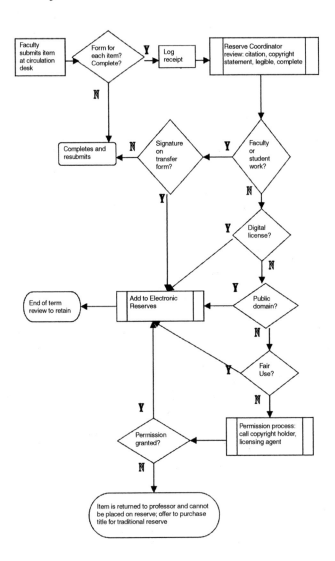

Determining Public Domain

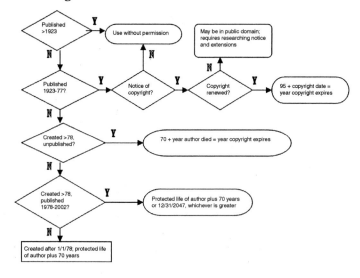

Determining Fair Use

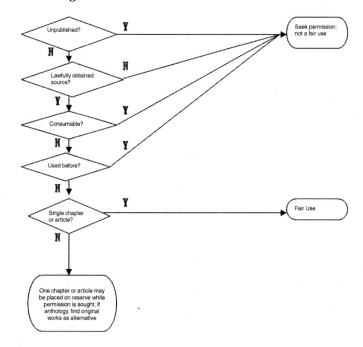

Scanning Checklist

Items are checked as they are completed. If the process must be interrupted, the checklist serves as a guide to what remains to be done.

____ Check **settings**
____ Scan general **copyright notice**
____ Scan **publisher's copyright information**
____ Scan **document**
____ **View** scanned pages
  ____ All pages included?
  ____ Legible?
____ **Crop** or **rotate** pages as necessary
____ **Optimize** file and **save** document
____ **Create** electronic reserves **record**
____ **Upload** file to electronic reserves system
____ **View** file from public side

Scanning Electronic Reserves Material Using Adobe Acrobat (with a Fujitsu ScanPartner 620C)

Getting Started

- Launch Adobe Acrobat by double-clicking the Acrobat shortcut on the desktop.
- Start with a clean, clear photocopy on 8.5 × 11-inch paper of the article you wish to put on Electronic Reserve. The photocopy should not have ragged edges or it will not feed properly through the scanner.
- Be certain that there are no dark borders on the sides of the pages that you are going to scan.
- Check the number of pages in the document. The automatic document feeder for the Fujitsu scanner can handle only 50 pages at a time. If your article has more than 50 pages, you'll need to scan in the first 50 pages, save the document, and then scan in the remainder, appending it to the end.
- To prevent occasional paper jams, fan the paper before loading.
- Lift the Balance Wire on the Automatic Document Feeder (ADF) and place the documents onto the paper chute face down, with the leading edge in the Auto Feeder entrance. Let the Balance Wire rest on top of the documents.

Title Page

- Each article to be scanned should have a title page. Right-click (or if using a Mac, click and hold the mouse button) here to <u>download the Wellesley College electronic reserves title page PDF form</u>. Choose Save this Link As and set the Format to Source (in Internet Explorer, choose Download Link to Disk).
- Fill in the title page with the necessary information: Author, Title, Publisher, Copyright Date, Course (e.g., BISC219), and Instructor.
- To fill out the title page click once on the area you desire to type in.
- Type in the desired information.
- The cursor can be moved in between fields in the form by pressing the Tab key or by clicking in the field using the mouse.
- Do not close the title page when you are done entering this information. It will become the first page of your document if it is open when you begin scanning.

Scanning the Image

- Make sure that the scanner is turned on and that no documents have been left on the flatbed of the scanner.
- Be sure that the e-reserves title page PDF form document is open.
- From the **File** menu select **Import** and then **Scan**.
- A dialog box will appear:

- In this window make the following selections from the pop-up menus:
  Device: ScanPartner 620C
  Format: Single sided
  Destination: Current Document (radio button)
- Click on the **Scan** button when all changes have been made.
- Place the documents **face down** on the document feeder tray.
- If you are using Windows 98, the ScanPartner 620C TWAIN Driver dialog box will appear:

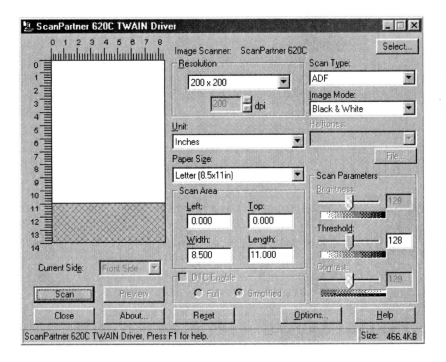

- Select or type in the following settings:
  Resolution: 200×200
  Scan Type: ADF
  Image Mode: Black & White
  Unit: Inches
  Paper Size: Letter (8.5×11 in)

- If you are using Windows 2000, a slightly different dialog box will appear:

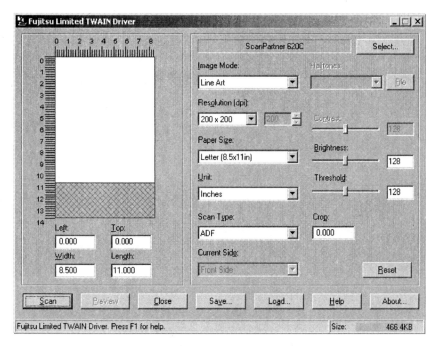

- Select or type in the following settings:
  Resolution: 200×200
  Scan Type: ADF
  Image Mode: Line Art
  Unit: Inches
  Paper Size: Letter (8.5×11 in)
- Click on the **Scan** button.
- A box will appear saying that the scanning is in progress. A progress box will also appear as each page is scanned.
- Wait while the scanning takes place. The article will take longer to scan if there are more pages. The following are approximate amounts of time that articles of certain lengths take to scan.
    <10 pages: 30 seconds
    20 pages: 1 minute
- When scanning is completed the Acrobat Scan Plug-in window will appear. (The scanner recognizes that it is out of paper and wishes to know if the article is completely scanned or if you have more pages to scan.)

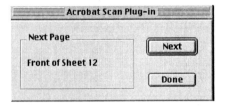

- Select **Done**.
- A window will appear saying that the pages are being transferred to Acrobat. Wait for the transfer to be completed.
- The document will appear in PDF format for viewing.

Viewing the Scanned Pages

- To view the entire page at once From the **View** menu, select **Fit in Window**.

Navigating within the Scanned Article

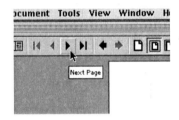

- Use arrow keys (in icon bar) as seen above to scroll through pages, making sure that all of the pages are aligned properly (all facing in the same direction).
- Some pages may need to be rotated if they are backwards or upside down (if so, see Rotating Pages section below; if not, skip the Rotating Pages section).
- Some pages may also need to be cropped if there are areas around the edges that you do not wish to appear when the article is printed (if so, see the Cropping Pages section; if not, then skip that section).

Rotating Pages

- From the **Document** menu select **Rotate Pages**. This can make documents easier to read on screen, but will not affect their orientation when printed.
- The Rotate Pages dialog box will appear.

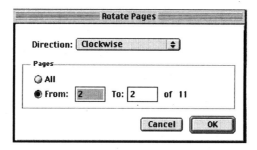

- From the **Direction** pull-down menu, select the desired direction of rotation (Clockwise or Counterclockwise).
- In the Pages section select the pages you want to rotate. **Note**: If you only want to rotate one page make sure that the page number (that of the page you wish to be rotated) appears in both the **From** and the **To** box. Highlighting them and then typing in the desired page number can change the page numbers in the boxes.
- Click **OK**.
- A window will appear asking you if you are sure you want to rotate the pages.

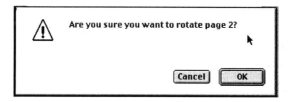

- Click **OK** to continue.

Cropping Pages

- Note that you cannot undo a crop operation. Cropping does not reduce file size, but can eliminate black borders from documents.
- From the **Document** menu select **Crop Pages**. (If you prefer, you can select the crop tool from the toolbar on the left, drag a cropping rectangle, and then double-click inside the rectangle.)
- The Crop Pages dialog box will appear.

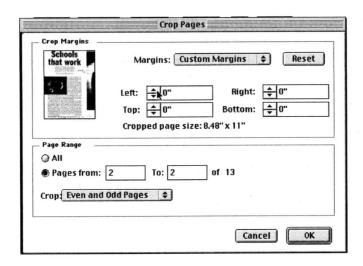

- Change the page margins by using the up and down arrow keys for each margin (left, right, top, bottom). If you used the crop tool to specify the page boundaries, select a handle at a corner of the cropping rectangle, and drag to the correct size.
- Make sure that **Pages from:** is selected.
- Click **OK**.

Saving the Document

- From the **File** menu select **Save As**, so that you may give the file a new name.
- Be sure the box next to **Optimize** is checked.
- Be sure to save the file on the PC desktop so that you can find it easily.
- Name your file with a .pdf extension (example: PLS327-UNV anquished.pdf). The file name can be no longer than 27 characters (excluding the ".pdf "). **You MUST include the .pdf extension!**
- The following format should be used in naming articles: **"Coursename#-title.pdf"**
  For example, "UN Vanquished" by Michael Barnett (Craig Murphy's Political Science 327 course): **POLS327-UNVanquished.pdf**
- Click on the **Save** button.

File Size

- Be sure to check the size of the PDF file.
- From the **File** menu, choose **Document Info–General**.

- Typically, a PDF file scanned at 200 dpi is roughly 60 Kbytes per page (i.e., a 20 page article should be roughly 1.2 MB in size).
- Uploading PDF files to FirstClass Electronic Reserves Drop Folders.
- Log in to FirstClass using your username and password.
- Open **Wellesley Conferences**, then **Campus-Wide Committees**, then find the **Electronic Reserves Drop** conference.
- Create a new FirstClass message, with a Subject line that follows the naming convention **Course# ArticleTitle Author**, and attach the PDF file to the message. For example, the Subject line for submitting the PDF file mentioned above could be Subject: **POLS327 UN Vanquished Barnett. Do not just upload the file.**
- The text of the FirstClass mail message should contain the full citation, e.g., Michael Barnett, "UN Vanquished," *Global Governance* (July/August 1999): 513-520.

How to Quit

To quit out of Adobe Acrobat, choose **File > Quit**.

Reproduced with permission from Wellesley College Information Services (Westfort, 2002).

These instructions assume all electronic journals to which the Library has access have been cataloged.

Searching Guide for Electronic Reserve Staff Members

I. E-Journals

Search the Library catalog for the title of the journal from which the article is taken. Ignore *a, and,* and *the* at the beginning. If a link to the journal is found, click through to the specific volume and year. Then locate the article. Cut and paste the URL into the electronic reserve record. If you must use a "search" option for the volume and year, there may not be a stable URL for the article. In this case, follow the links to the last stable URL, then cut and paste that into the record. The professor and students should be referred to the instructions for "Accessing Full-text Electronic Reserves."

II. Journal Home Page

If no full-text is found using **E-Journals**, search the Web to see if the journal has a web site. Before linking, verify that articles can be accessed directly. If a username and password are required, contact the Electronic Reserve Permissions Coordinator.

III. Electronic Books

The full-text of some books are available electronically. First, search the Library catalog for the book title. Ignore *a, and,* and *the*. If a link exists, click through to the chapter, then cut and paste the URL into the electronic reserve record. If a stable link does not exist to the chapter, use the last stable URL to the table of contents or a "search" option. If the book has not yet been cataloged, it may have recently been added to the e-book database(s). Follow the same procedure to search each available database.

Permission Letter for Electronic Reserve

[Letterhead with return address]

[Date]

[Copyright owner address]

Dear Copyright Owner:

A faculty member at [Name of institution] would like to place the following material on the library's electronic reserve system:

[Citation]

This request is for:

[Semester, year]
[Department]
[Course number]
[Course title]
[Section number, if applicable]
[Professor name]
[#] Enrolled students

Access to the electronic reserve system is restricted to students only by [describe whether IP-validated, password, etc.].

I would appreciate your permission for my request on behalf of the faculty and students. If you require any additional information, please contact me at:

[Reserve Coordinator contact information]

Please sign this agreement below [or on the back] and return it to me in the enclosed envelope.

Sincerely,

[Signature]

Permission granted for the use of the material as described above:

Name & Title: _____

Affiliation:_____

Date:_____

Notice to Faculty that an Item Cannot Be Placed on Electronic Reserve

[Date]

Dear [Professor's name],

The Library has attempted to secure copyright clearance for one of the items you submitted for electronic reserve:

[Citation]

We have been unsuccessful because

_____ The copyright holder has denied permission.
_____ We received no response to our requests.
_____ The royalty fees were excessively high.

To remain in compliance with copyright law, we cannot include this item in electronic reserve. Please contact the Library if you would like assistance searching for a suitable replacement. We regret the inconvenience.

Sincerely,

[Signature]

[Reserve Coordinator name]

Electronic Reserve Coordinator

[Institution name]

Retain or Release Reserve Material Notice

COURSE NUMBER _____ SEMESTER _____

PROFESSOR _____

Materials on electronic course reserve are not automatically retained from term to term without written notice from the professor. Items that comply with copyright law may be retained. Upon notice to retain materials, the Library will again seek copyright clearance. If permission is denied or the royalty fees are excessive, the item will be removed from electronic reserve and you will be notified.

Please

_____ retain
_____ remove

all electronic reserve materials for my course for

_____ Fall
_____ Spring
_____ Summer

semester.

Signature: _____ Date: _____

Instructions for Retaining or Removing Materials on Electronic Reserve

Six weeks before the end of a semester, the Library will send Retain/Release forms to professors who have items on electronic reserve. Routine releasing of reserve items will begin on the last day of each semester. Items requested to be released or retained will be processed first, followed by all remaining electronic reserve items.

If materials will be retained

- Verify the course number and the professor's name at the top of the request form; update the term and year
- Update the electronic course reserve system
  - Change the expiration date to the last day of the next term
  - Verify information and update if needed

If materials will be removed

- Update the electronic course reserve system to remove access to the item (or unlink the record)
- Record action on form and file

Student Guide to Using Electronic Course Reserves

Electronic Reserves are supplementary course materials available electronically, including digitized text, image, audio, and video materials. Class notes, exams, syllabi, homework, student papers, copies of articles, and other items are examples of the many types of things that your professor may place on reserve at the library. These materials are accessible from your computer or library computers, 24 hours a day, 7 days a week.

To access electronic reserve materials

1. You will need the Adobe Acrobat Reader to access the readings. Acrobat is loaded on the Library computers, or you may download it for free from the Adobe web site at: http://www.adobe.com/products/acrobat/readstep.html. Click on the "Get Acrobat Reader Free" text near the bottom of the page. You will then receive step-by-step instructions to download the software. RealPlayer is freely available for viewing and/or listening to other media; see http://www.real.com/.
2. Select "Electronic Course Reserve" from the Library web site.
3. Electronic reserve materials are limited to students and faculty, so if you are accessing the system from off-campus, you will be prompted to enter your current Library ID number.
4. Search for your particular course using your professor's last name or the course number.
5. You will then see the list of titles your professor has submitted.
6. There will be a line that indicates this is an online item. Click on the link to access the file.
7. After you access the file, the readings may be printed or read onscreen, or other media may be played using RealPlayer.

Course Reserve Satisfaction Survey

Let us know how we're doing.

Please circle a number on each of the following rating scales.

1. How easy was it to use course reserve materials?

Very difficult   1   2   3   4   5   Very easy

2. How available were the materials for your course?

Unavailable   1   2   3   4   5   Readily available

3. How satisfied were you with the quality of the material?

Not satisfied   1   2   3   4   5   Very satisfied

4. How helpful were the staff members?

Not helpful   1   2   3   4   5   Very helpful

Please answer the questions below. Additional comments are welcome.

Rank: ____ undergraduate   ____ faculty
         ____ graduate   ____ other staff

References and Resources

REFERENCES

Agreement on Guidelines for Classroom Copying in Not-for-Profit Educational Institutions with Respect to Books and Periodicals. (1976, March). Available: http://www.musiclibraryassoc.org/Copyright/guidebks.htm.

Algenio, E. R. (2002). A how-to guide for electronic reserves; or, if I knew then what I know now. *Journal of Interlibrary Loan, Document Delivery & Information Supply*, *12*(3), 1-12.

Alliance for Nonprofit Management. (n.d.). *Strategic Planning*. Available: http://www.allianceonline.org/Test_FAQs/sp_main.html.

Association of American Publishers. (n.d.). *Conferences & Publications–Publications: Guidelines for Classroom Copying*. Available: http://www.publishers.org/conference/copyguide.cfm.

Association of Research Libraries Collections & Access Issues Task Force. (2002, December). Collections & access for the 21st-century scholar: Changing roles of research libraries. *ARL Bimonthly Report 225*. Available: http://www.arl.org/newsltr/225/main.html.

Avery, E. F., Dahlin, T., & Carver, D. A. (2001). *Staff Development: A Practical Guide (3rd ed.)*. Chicago, IL: American Library Association.

Bodi, R. F. (2003, March 14). Re: Copyright Education/Interpretation of Law. Posting to http://www.cni.org/forums/cni-copyright/cni-copyright.html.

CENDI Copyright Task Group. (2002, January 2). *Frequently Asked Questions About Copyright*. Available: http://www.dtic.mil/cendi/publications/00-3copyright.html.

[Haworth co-indexing entry note]: "References and Resources." Driscoll, Lori. Co-published simultaneously in *Journal of Interlibrary Loan, Document Delivery & Information Supply* (The Haworth Information Press, an imprint of The Haworth Press, Inc.) Vol. 14, No. 1, 2003, pp. 87-91; and: *Electronic Reserve: A Manual and Guide for Library Staff Members* (Lori Driscoll) The Haworth Information Press, an imprint of The Haworth Press, Inc., 2003, pp. 87-91. Single or multiple copies of this article are available for a fee from The Haworth Document Delivery Service [1-800-HAWORTH, 9:00 a.m. - 5:00 p.m. (EST). E-mail address: docdelivery@haworthpress.com].

10.1300/J110v14n01_08   *87*

College Savings Bank v. Florida Prepaid Postsecondary Ed. Expense Bd. (98-149) 131 F.3d 353. (1998). Available: http://www.usdoj.gov/osg/briefs/1998/0responses/98-0149.resp.opp.html.

Copyright Management Center at Indiana University-Purdue University Indianapolis. (2000, April 24). *Electronic Reserves and Copyright at IUPUI.* Available: http://www.iupui.edu/~copyinfo/ereserves.html.

Creative Commons. (2003, January 15). *Introduction.* Available: http://creativecommons.org/.

Crews, K. D. (2002). *New Copyright Law for Distance Education: The Meaning and Importance of the TEACH Act.* From the American Library Association Web site. Available: http://www.ala.org/washoff/teach.html.

Crews, K. D. (2000). *Copyright Essentials for Librarians and Educators.* Chicago: American Library Association.

Eldred v. Ashcroft, No. 01-618 U.S. (2003). Available: http://www.supremecourtus.gov/opinions/02pdf/01-618.pdf.

Final Report to the Commissioner on the Conclusion of the Conference on Fair Use. (1998, November). Available: http://www.uspto.gov/web/offices/dcom/lia/confu/confurep.htm.

Gassaway, L. N. (2001). *Copyright Law in the Digital Age: Course Materials.* From the University of North Carolina Katherine R. Everett Law Library Web site. Available: http://www.unc.edu/~unclng/gasaway.htm.

Geller, P. E. (Ed.). (1993). *International Copyright Law and Practice.* New York: Matthew Bender.

Howe, D. (Ed.). (2002, July 16). *The Free On-line Dictionary of Computing.* Available: http://www.foldoc.org/.

Jensen, M. B. (1993, March). Electronic reserves and copyright. *Computers in Libraries, 13*(3), 40-45.

Jones, S. (2002, September 15). The Internet goes to college: How students are living in the future with today's technology. *Pew Internet & American Life Project.* Available: http://www.pewinternet.org/reports/toc.asp?Report=71.

JSTOR. (2002, February 14). *JSTOR: Mission and Goals.* Available: http://www.jstor.org/about/mission.html.

Kristof, C. (1999). *SPEC Kit 245 Electronic Reserves Operations in ARL Libraries.* Washington, D.C.: Association of Research Libraries.

Marley, J. L. (1999, September). Guidelines favoring fair use: An analysis of legal interpretations affecting higher education. *Journal of Academic Librarianship, 25*(5), 367-371.

Melamut, S. J., Thibodeau, P. L., & Albright, E. D. (2000). Fair use or not fair use: That is the electronic reserves question? *Journal of Interlibrary Loan, Document Delivery & Information Supply, 11*(1), 3-28.

Model Policy Concerning College and University Photocopying for Classroom, Research and Library Reserve Use. (1982). Available: http://www.cni.org/docs/infopols/ALA.html-mpup.

Nackerud, S. (1999, April). E-Reserves: Home grown vs. turnkey. *ACRL Ninth National Conference, Detroit, Michigan.* Available: http://www.ala.org/acrl/nackerud.pdf.

Niederlander, M. (1998). Core competencies. LibrarySupportStaff.com. Available: http://www.librarysupportstaff.com/4competency3.html.

Norman, D. A. (1997). *The Invisible Computer.* Cambridge, MA: MIT Press. Available: http://www.jnd.org/dn.mss/being_analog.html.

North Carolina State University. (2003, January). *The TEACH Toolkit.* Available: http://www.lib.ncsu.edu/scc/legislative/teachkit/.

Ochoa, T. (2002, December 9). Re: Library Electronic Reserves. Posting to http://www.cni.org/forums/cni-copyright/cni-copyright.html.

Okerson, A. (2001, September 1). Wanted: A model for e-reserves. *Library Journal,* 56-58.

Project Gutenberg. (2002, November 13). *About Project Gutenberg.* Available: http://promo.net/pg/.

Radcliffe, M. (1999). Types of works protected by copyright. In the *Multimedia Law and Business Handbook.* Available: http://www.laderapress.com/laderapress/noname2.html.

Rosedale, J. *Electronic Reserves Clearinghouse: Links and Materials on the Web.* Available: http://www.mville.edu/Administration/staff/Jeff_Rosedale/.

Rosedale, J. (Ed.). (2002). *Managing Electronic Reserves.* Chicago: American Library Association.

Rosedale, J. (2001, August 19). Overview. *SPEC Kit 217 Transforming Libraries: Issues and Innovations in Electronic Reserves.* Washington, D.C.: Association of Research Libraries. Available: http://www.arl.org/transform/eres/over.html.

Rudenstine, N. L., & Shulman, J. (2003). *ARTstor: Overview and History.* Available: http://www.mellon.org/programs/otheractivities/ArtSTOR/Content.htm.

Sellen, M., & Hazard, B. (2001). User assessment of electronic reserves and implications for digital libraries. *Journal of Interlibrary Loan, Document Delivery & Information Supply, 12*(1), 73-83.

Soete, G. (1996). *SPEC Kit 217 Transforming Libraries: Issues and Innovations in Electronic Reserves*. Washington, D.C.: Association of Research Libraries.

Tampa Bay Library Consortium (TBLC). (2000). Core competencies. Available: http://snoopy.tblc.lib.fl.us/training/competencies.shtml.

Technology, Education, and Copyright Harmonization Act of 2002. Educational Use Copyright Exemption. Pub. L. No. 107-273, Sec. 13301. Available: http://www.copyright.gov/legislation/pl107-273.html.

United States Copyright Office. (2001, June). *Circular 92: Copyright Law of the United States of America and Related Laws Contained in Title 17 of the United States Code*. Available: http://www.copyright.gov/title17/circ92.pdf.

United States Copyright Office. (2000, August). *Circular 15a. Duration of Copyright: Provisions of the Law Dealing with the Length of Copyright Protection*. Available: http://www.copyright.gov/circs/circ15a.html.

United States Copyright Office. (1999, June). *Circular 3: Copyright Notice*. Available: http://www.loc.gov/copyright/circs/circ03.html.

United States General Accounting Office. (2001, September). GAO-01-811 *State Immunity in Infringement Actions*, p. 2.

United States Senate Report Number 94-473 (1976) p. 63. Available: http://biotech.law.lsu.edu/cases/immunity/GAO_d01811.pdf.

Westfort, M. (2002). Scanning electronic reserves material using Adobe Acrobat (with a Fujitsu ScanPartner 620C). *Wellesley College Information Services: Computing Documentation*. Available: http://www.wellesley.edu/Computing/Acrobat/E-Reserves/e-reserve-scanning-fujitsu.html.

World Intellectual Property Organization (WIPO). (2002, December). *Intellectual Property on the Internet: A Survey of Issues*. Available: http://ecommerce.wipo.int/survey/html/3.html#3a.

LICENSING AGENTS

Access Copyright (The Canadian Copyright Licensing Agency)
One Yonge Street, Suite 1900, Toronto, Ontario M5E 1E5 Canada
Phone: + 1 416 868 1620
http://www.accesscopyright.ca/

Copyright Clearance Center (CCC)
222 Rosewood Drive, Danvers, MA 01923 USA
Phone: 978-750-8400
http://www.copyright.com/

International Federation of Reproduction Rights Organisations
Rue du Prince Royal 87, B-1050 Brussels Belgium
Phone: + 32 2 551 08 99
Directory of Member Organizations at:
http://www.ifrro.org/members/index.html

LISTSERVS

ARL-ERESERVE

http://www.cni.org/Hforums/arl-ereserve/about.html

"ARL has established this list to provide a forum for discussion of issues surrounding management of electronic reserve within libraries. New technologies can be the catalyst for transforming instructional support. This transformation raises technical, policy and intellectual property questions."

CNI-COPYRIGHT

http://www.cni.org/forums/cni-copyright/cni-copyright.html

"Issues related to copyright, intellectual property rights, and public access to information in the digital age are at the forefront of public debate in the twenty-first century. [The Coalition for Networked Information's] Copyright Forum provides an open space for discussion of these topics as they relate to the networked information community."

LIBLICENSE

http://www.library.yale.edu/~llicense/index.shtml

"LIBLICENSE-L is a moderated list for the discussion of issues related to the licensing of digital information by academic and research libraries . . . This list is designed to assist librarians and others concerned with the licensing of information in digital format in dealing with some of the unique challenges faced by this new medium."

Glossary

Analog

"An analog device is one in which the representation of information corresponds to its physical structure. . . . A phonograph recording is analog: It works by recreating the variations in sound energy by wiggles and depth of the groove. In a tape recording, the strength of the magnetic field on the tape varies in analogous fashion to the sound energy variations" (Norman, 1997).

Attribution

Acknowledgement of a particular person as the creator of a work–author, artist, editor, etc.

Citation

A thorough acknowledgment of the source of information, including author, title of work, and date of publication.

Collective Works (Anthologies)

"A 'collective work' is one in which a number of contributions that are separate and independent works in themselves are assembled into a collective whole. Examples of collective works include periodicals (such as magazines and journals), encyclopedias, and anthologies. A single copyright notice applicable to the collective work as a whole serves to indicate protection for all the contributions in the collective work, except for ad-

---

[Haworth co-indexing entry note]: "Glossary." Driscoll, Lori. Co-published simultaneously in *Journal of Interlibrary Loan, Document Delivery & Information Supply* (The Haworth Information Press, an imprint of The Haworth Press, Inc.) Vol. 14, No. 1, 2003, pp. 93-97; and: *Electronic Reserve: A Manual and Guide for Library Staff Members* (Lori Driscoll) The Haworth Information Press, an imprint of The Haworth Press, Inc., 2003, pp. 93-97. Single or multiple copies of this article are available for a fee from The Haworth Document Delivery Service [1-800-HAWORTH, 9:00 a.m. - 5:00 p.m. (EST). E-mail address: docdelivery@haworth press.com].

10.1300/J110v14n01_09

vertisements, regardless of the ownership of copyright in the individual contributions and whether they have been published previously" (U.S. Copyright Office, June 1999, *Circular 3: Copyright Notice*).

Copyright

Copyright is a form of protection provided by the laws of the United States to the authors of original works including literary, dramatic, musical, artistic, and certain other intellectual works. Copyright protection is automatic once an original work of authorship is fixed in a tangible medium of expression, now known or later developed; e.g., written, filmed, recorded. It does not require that a copyright notice be placed on the work, that the work is published, or that the work is deposited or registered with the Copyright Office or any other body (CENDI).

Copyright Designation or Notice

A copyright notice is an identifier placed on copies of the work to inform the world of copyright ownership. © 1999 Jane Doe or © 1999 X.Y.Z. Records, Inc. This may also be combined with the copyright statement.

Copyright Owner

With respect to any one of the exclusive rights comprised in a copyright, refers to the owner of that particular right. Copyright in a work vests initially in the author or authors of the work. However, the author may assign some or all of his or her rights to another, who then becomes the owner of the rights assigned. Under the U.S. Copyright Law, for a work made for hire, that is a work prepared by an employee within the scope of employment or a specially ordered or commissioned work, the employer or other person for whom the work was prepared is considered the author (CENDI).

Copyright Statement

The copyright owner's copyright notice and any statement about use of materials, permissions contact information, or transfer of rights.

Courseware

Courseware is derived from the words "course" and "software." Although it can be applied broadly to include any method of delivering any part of a course via the computer, the term is used more narrowly here to describe software packages that have been specifically developed to deliver course materials over the Internet.

Course Packs

These are collections of materials photocopied by commercial copy shops. The copy shop obtains permissions for the use of copyrighted material. The royalty fees and other charges are included in the cost of the course pack paid by each student.

Digital

The process of digitization converts materials into binary form that can be transmitted over a network, copied, and stored. Materials can be text, sound, images, computer programs, and audiovisual works (WIPO, p. 29).

Fair Use

Exemptions to the exclusive rights provided by copyright, as in copying for purposes such as criticism comment, news reporting, teaching (including multiple copies for classroom use), scholarship, or research. The fair use limitation identifies four factors that should be evaluated on a case-by-case basis in order to determine if a specific use is "fair." There is no right number of words, lines or notes that qualify as a fair use (CENDI).

Fixed

A work is "fixed" in a tangible medium of expression when it is recorded in a physical medium (analog or digital), by or under the authority of the author, and is sufficiently permanent or stable to permit it to be perceived, reproduced, or otherwise communicated for a period of more than transitory duration. A work consisting of sounds, images, or both, that are being transmitted, is "fixed" for purposes of this title if a fixation of the work is being made simultaneously with its transmission (U.S. Copyright Law).

Infringement

Unauthorized use of a copyrighted work is an infringement unless the use is outside the exclusive rights provided by the copyright law, or unless the use is covered by one of the limitations on the exclusive right, such as fair use (CENDI).

Integrated Library Automation System

An automated system that includes various modules for library operations, such as acquisitions, circulation, cataloging, serials, and an OPAC (Online Public Access Catalog) that function together by sharing information.

IP Authentication

The verification of a person's identity through the Internet protocol address, like a signature. Authentication verifies the source of a transmission.

Lawfully Obtained Copy

A faculty member or library should have obtained the copy through purchase, licensing, or interlibrary loan.

License

A license is a contract between a copyright owner or the owner's authorized agent, such as a third party vendor, and another party giving permission to use a work, usually with the payment of a fee or royalty.

Masthead

The place in a periodical or newspaper that gives the title and pertinent details of ownership, advertising, and subscriptions; the notice of copyright may be located here.

Permission

Permission is an agreement from a copyright owner allowing another party to exercise one or more of the exclusive rights provided the copyright owner under the Copyright Law. Permission may also be referred to as a Copyright Release (CENDI).

Public Domain

Materials on which the copyright has expired, for which the author released copyrights to the public, or that are produced by the federal government.

Publication

Publication is the distribution of copies of a work to the public by sale or other transfer of ownership or by rental, lease, or lending. Distributing copies to a group of persons for purposes of further distribution, public performance, or public display, constitutes publication. A public performance or display of a work does not of itself constitute publication (CENDI).

Recto

The opposite of verso, this is the right-hand page in a bound work, usually given an uneven page number. The title page and first pages of other major parts of the book are printed here.

Registration

The registration of a claim to copyright or the renewed and extended term of copyright.

Royalty

A payment to the rights holder for use of a copyrighted work.

URL

The uniform resource locator (URL) is a standardized way of specifying the location of a web page. URLs are the current form of address used on the World Wide Web.

Verso

The verso is the left-hand or backside page of a bound work, usually given an even page number. The copyright statement, publishers' imprint, publication date, ISBN, and cataloging in publication (CIP) information is usually printed on the verso of the title page.

Index

AALL (American Association of Law Libraries), 49-50
Access- and use-related issues, 48
Access Copyright, CANCOPY licenses, 34,90
Accountability competencies, 10
Agents, licensing, 33-34,90-91
"Agreement on Guidelines for Classroom Copying in Not-for-Profit Educational Institutions with Respect to Books and Periodicals," 45-46
ALA (American Library Association), 46,49-50
Analog and analog devices, 93
Anthologies (collective works), 93-94
ARL (Association of Research Libraries), 4,15,17,49-51
ARL-ERESERVE (listserv), 91
Art Libraries Society of North America, 49-50
ARTstor project, 51-52
Assessments, 24-25
Attribution and note issues, 47-48,93
Authentication, 96

Bibliographies. *See* References and resources

CANCOPY licenses, Access Copyright, 34
CCC (Copyright Clearance Center), 9,33-34,90-91
CENDI Copyright Task Group, 35-36, 87-88
Centralization, workflow, 29

Checklists, samples of, 68-69,72-80
Citations, 93
Clarification, procedures, 28-29
CNI-COPYRIGHT (listserv), 91
Collective works (anthologies), 93-94
Communication skills, 10,12-13
Competencies, staff. *See also* Staffing considerations
  accountability, 10,12
  communication skills, 10,12-13
    oral, 10,12-13
    written, 10,13
  flexibility, 11,13
  innovation, 11,13
  interpersonal, 11,13
  leadership, 14
  organizational, 11
  personal and educational development, 11,14
  problem-solving skills, 11-12,14
  resource management, 12,14-15
  service attitudes, 12,15
  teamwork, 12
  technological expertise, 12,15
CONFU (Conference on Fair Use), 46-48
Coordinators, competencies of, 9-10
Copyright-related issues. *See also* under individual topics
  CENDI Copyright Task Group and, 35-36,87-88
  copyright-specific definitions
    of copyright, 94
    of copyright designation notices, 94
    of copyright owners, 94
    of copyright statements, 94
  fair use considerations, 40-41, 45-53,95